MINISTRY NOW
New Approaches for a Changing Church

Martin Kennedy

VERITAS

First published 2006 by
Veritas Publications
7/8 Lower Abbey Street
Dublin 1
Ireland
Email publications@veritas.ie
Website www.veritas.ie

ISBN 1 84730 003 0
978 1 84730 003 4

Copyright © Martin Kennedy, 2006

10 9 8 7 6 5 4 3 2 1

The material in this publication is protected by copyright law. Except as may be permitted by law, no part of the material may be reproduced (including by storage in a retrieval system) or transmitted in any form or by any means, adapted, rented or lent without the written permission of the copyright owners. Applications for permissions should be addressed to the publisher.

W.B. Yeats' 'The Fiddler of Dooney' appears with permission of AP Watt Ltd on behalf of Michael B. Yeats (pp. 61–2).

A catalogue record for this book
is available from the British Library.

Printed in the Republic of Ireland
by Betaprint Dublin

Veritas books are printed on paper made from the wood pulp of managed forests. For every tree felled, at least one tree is planted, thereby renewing natural resources.

CONTENTS

Introduction   5

Part One Ministry Perspectives

1	Stories to start	11
2	A spirit hopeful and troubled	17
3	Down in the valley	27
4	'Find the traces of the Spirit'	38
5	Travellers together	46
6	The Spirit among the 'A's	52
7	The Spirit among the 'B's	60
8	The Spirit among the 'C's	65
9	Mission impermanent – not impossible!	71
10	Status anxiety	75

Part Two Ministry Approaches

Section 1: Evangelisation

11	Into the deep	83
12	A pastoral structure for evangelisation	88

13	Horses for courses	94
14	Evangelisation as dialogue	98
15	Sunday mass	106
16	Our music of the gospel	113
17	An evangelisation moment with parents	122
18	Evangelising pre-teens	127

Section 2: Justice

19	Works as well as words	131
20	Reaching out to the young	135
21	Listening at the margins	138

Section 3: Communion

22	The priest and managing ministry	144
23	Parish leadership groups	150
24	Structure and spirituality for communion	156
25	Organising for action	162
26	Employing pastoral workers	168
27	'Expectant' leadership	171

References   174

Introduction

This book is mainly a collection of short pieces that I have written over the years for *Intercom* and other magazines. The pieces are reflections 'on the move' where I try to describe and think out loud about ministry in the midst of my involvement. They come out of a context of working with others and are intended to go back into that context, not as finished articles, but as contributions to an ongoing story of pastoral trial and error.

I hope they provide some raw material for ministry and theology, in that they are the honest reflections of a layman at the coalface of ministry in this turn-of-century Irish church. That leaves plenty of room for mistakes!

Even though they are personal reflections I believe they do represent something of the *sensus fidelium*, the common sense of the people of God. I have used this material a good deal in working with people across the country and, generally, I found it resonated with them.

The chapters are grouped in two main sections. The first offers a general perspective on ministry in contemporary Irish culture. Its fundamental thrust (both in terms of church and culture) is hopeful, and I try to give a reasoned account for that hope. However, it is also troubled. I see the issue of child abuse and our response to it as a sign of a deep malaise in the church, requiring fundamental repentance and conversion.

The second section looks at some practical approaches to ministry and is in three parts. This section takes its structure from Pope John Paul's letter 'At the Beginning of the New Millennium', where he identifies three pastoral priorities for the local churches at this time. Holiness (fostering our experience of God), charity (a commitment to justice for marginalised people at local and global levels) and communion (all in the church working together in a way that cherishes our mutual giftedness).

In part one of this section I look at approaches to evangelisation which I believe can be effective in this time and place. In part two I look at some approaches to the work of justice. In part three I look at concrete ways of people working together with a particular emphasis on the workings of parish leadership groups. The treatment of the different areas is very uneven. I was surprised at how little material I had for the section on justice. At a time of fundamental (and I think welcome) social change in regard to wealth and population there is a great deal more to be addressed in this area.

I am conscious that I am only one among a great many involved in ministry action and reflection. We do not all share the same convictions and approaches, but I do think we need to talk to each other honestly and respectfully. Somewhere among us now the Spirit is active. Some among us are digging in the pastoral fields where we will

INTRODUCTION

find gold; others are digging where we will not. I cannot know for certain which group I belong to but this I do know: there are at least some areas I am pointing to, claiming gold is to be found there, that will be proven wrong. There are some people digging where I think there is nothing to be found who will likewise prove me wrong. So, I think it makes sense that we diggers talk to each other. To use another metaphor, we are beggars searching for bread. We can tell one another where we have found it and where we have not. That way we might all have a chance to eat!

PART ONE

MINISTRY PERSPECTIVES

CHAPTER

1   Stories to start

There were just two of us in the hotel meeting room: the parish priest and I. We had organised a talk for young parents on the Primary School religion programme. Our purpose was evangelisation – we wanted the parents to get a sense of the good news of the gospel for their children and for themselves. A written invitation had gone out to hundreds of homes. The night had been promoted at all the weekend masses. And nobody turned up. The hotel manager came in to us as we surveyed the empty rows of seats. 'Don't worry,' he said, 'I won't charge you for the room.'

    Looking back now we can laugh at that moment, but it didn't feel funny at the time. Our hearts were down in our boots – and it wasn't for the first time. Some months earlier we organised a similar night in the day chapel as part of our regular theology programme. With sixteen hundred Primary School children in the parish we had a very big target group of parents. On the night, very few of our regular participants turned up for the talk – they told us afterwards that they had felt the night wasn't for them

MINISTRY NOW

– and just three parents came out of a possible three thousand. One tenth of one per cent!

In the frustration and humiliation of these moments our first questions were about the parents: 'What is wrong with them that they won't come to what we have organised for them? Have they any religious sense at all? Have they any care for their responsibilities as parents?'

However, when we regrouped to review and plan, we knew in our hearts these were not the right questions. The real questions were: 'What was wrong with what we were offering or with how we were offering it that we didn't succeed in attracting the parents? What is it that we need to do differently?'

A few years later and we were back to the day chapel with the same target group of parents and for the same purpose. By this time we had developed a series of programmes, one of which was for the parents of junior infants. On this occasion our problem was that we did not have enough chairs. So, what was different? Why did one initiative flounder while another flourished? Describing the difference is easy; explaining it will take the rest of this book. Basically we shifted the focus of the night from formal education to celebration. We invited the parents and families to come along to a Christmas prayer service and celebration marking the Junior Infants' completion of their first ever term in school. The celebration included:

- Showing on a large-screen video footage of the children in their classroom doing their religion programme
- A prayer service made up of songs and prayers that the children had learned

- A small ritual around a Christmas tree where each child was called by name
- A talk on the relevance of the religion programme to the development of the children and the role that the parents could play
- A party for the children and tea for the parents.

The invitation to a religious celebration to mark their children's first term in school sparked the imagination of the parents. The invitation to a religious talk did not. I am deeply struck by the two contrasting images here – the empty room and the packed room. What is it saying to us? Is it something about the parents that turns them from evangelising moments, or is it something about how we imagine and organise these moments?

***

Another story. I was at a parish meeting of ministry group representatives. We were discussing a common problem – the scarcity of volunteers for our various activities. We had tried different strategies of recruitment but these had not worked. We were bemoaning people's lack of energy and enthusiasm for what we were doing. Sometime later I was working with the parish adult religious education group. We had a visiting homilist at the weekend liturgies – one of a number booked over the year. At all the masses she spoke on the issue of domestic violence and posed the challenge – 'What is the Christian community in this town doing to care for women who experience violence in their own homes?' Normally there would be a short meeting after each mass in the day chapel, providing an opportunity for a group conversation with the homilist. But the folk who came back this time weren't looking for a conversation. They wanted action. They had a quiet but powerful energy for the issue raised and they wanted to be part of a response to that issue. They challenged us on what we were going to do in the parish.

Of course, we hadn't a clue! We had not expected this kind of response and had no plans for follow-up. We took their names and promised to get in touch. The questions we were left with initially were: 'What are we going to do with these people? We don't know anything about this issue – what can we do?' We were feeling helpless until we changed the question to: 'Who can we bring in to equip these people to engage in the kind of activities they are looking to be part of?' A telephone call to a crisis support agency clarified that they could identify a support programme that could be run in our town and, further, that they could provide the training for the volunteers willing to run that programme. Our task from there was simple. We brought together the people who had energy for providing a support programme with those who had the resources to equip them. The programme took off from there and is still running ten years later.

Again I am struck by the contrasts. In the first scenario with the ministry groups our underlying question was, 'Where do we find energy for the programmes?' In the second scenario, after the weekend homilies, our question was very different: 'Where do we find programmes for the energy?' In the first case we were looking for people to fit our systems, in the second systems to fit our people.

***

A third story. After the visit of the relics of St Therese our pastoral council decided that it would be a good time to initiate an annual Novena to St Therese. The plan was to call a public meeting open to anyone who had energy for the Novena. Their task would be to imagine and plan the features and organisation of the Novena – to take responsibility to make it happen. Because of the huge interest that the visit had generated we were confident of a very good response. Yet on the night only six people turned up. 'The same old faces!' they said, and they looked seriously at the question of whether they should abandon the task and go home.

But they didn't go home. Instead they set about organising the Novena in a way that created practical tasks for a range of volunteers – hand-delivering invitations into neighbours' homes, ushering at the different services, preparation of church décor and so on. A few weeks later at the weekend masses a volunteer stand was erected at the back of the church. People were invited to sign up for a task of their choice. About one hundred did.

On the first night of the Novena a man and his son were walking to the session. 'I suppose there won't be a big crowd at this,' said the father. When they arrived they had to push their way through the crowds. Fifteen hundred people had packed the church. By the second night people were coming half an hour early to get good seats!

Again I find the contrasts striking and evocative. Six people found a way of gathering one hundred who in turn gathered fifteen hundred. Only a few had the energy or the confidence to sit with the question of the Novena, to start with a blank sheet and create something. A larger group had the energy to work with practical tasks, once those tasks were defined. And a much larger group again had the energy to participate in the event itself.

Over the years I have stumbled into many experiences like these. I have found them deeply heartening. They have left me with a strong conviction about the possibilities of mission in contemporary culture. But they have also challenged me to re-examine a lot of my assumptions; to look at the possibility that difficulties in ministry might have more to do with how we ministers go about it than with the people we seek to minister to.

CHAPTER

2 A spirit hopeful and troubled

I turned fifty this summer. I have spent more than thirty years involved in some form of church ministry. So in this personal mid-life moment, which is at the same time a moment of great trauma for the Irish church, I find myself in a reflective mood. Any thoughtful Christian has to struggle with questions such as, 'How are we doing with our mission in today's world? What must we do to move forward with energy and effectiveness?' I face these questions in a spirit that is both hopeful and troubled.

A hopeful spirit
I believe that core to any Christian discernment is a search for concrete signs of life and hope, even in very difficult circumstances. A search rooted in our faith that in the midst of everything the Spirit of God is working. And because God's Spirit is working in the present, there is evidence to be sought out and recognised. Evidence that can give us heart and direction for the future.

I can't find that evidence on my own. Christian discernment is a community activity. I have often heard Fr Mícheál Liston say, 'We are beggars telling other beggars where we found bread'. I love this image for our efforts at building and sharing our wisdom. We all bring something of value, but we are needy and we need each other. None of us knows it all.

I am one of many thousands of people who have struggled with ministry, who search for heart and hope for the future. We are in every parish the length and breadth of the country. We are a mixed bunch – men, women, young, old – involved in different ways, sometimes holding very different viewpoints on the kind of church and society we would like to see. Some of us are priests or religious. Most of us, like me, are lay people. What we all have in common is simply that we have been touched deeply by our faith. It has been very good news for us. We would like that same faith to be good news for others. There beats within each of us a missionary heart. It is to this heart that I write.

For most of us, while we feel the call to share our faith in some way, we also feel fragile and uncertain about responding. We are living in the early years of the third millennium, painfully aware that this is a changing and often difficult time and place for faith and church. We are aware too of the challenge of the late Pope John Paul II for us all to get involved in very concrete, planned ways of bringing the good news of the gospel to the society we live in. 'Let us go forward in hope,' he said. 'The new millennium is opening up before the Church like a vast ocean upon which we shall venture relying on the help of Christ.' *(At the Beginning of the New Millennium,* n. 58)

What does this challenge feel like for us? How do our hearts respond? Do they lift at the prospect of reaching out to the people around us, or do they sink? I think it is hugely important that we stay attuned to the state of our hearts, that we notice the patterns in what lifts us and what knocks us. I believe there are ways of viewing and going about our mission that can give us a sense of hope and energy; that can release in us a sense of adventure and excitement. I believe that fun, laughter and enjoyment should all be part of the normal experience of our church involvement. Not all the time – there will be frustrations, disappointments and conflicts. However, I believe that it should, and could, be normal for us to laugh when we are together; normal for us to look forward to our meetings, to enjoy our praying together, our planning, our activities, our reviews, our successes – even our failures.

Likewise I think there are ways of viewing and going about our mission that have the opposite effect on us; that unnecessarily drain us of hope and sap our energy, killing off our enthusiasm. When this happens it is an immense loss. Not just for the gospel and the church but for ourselves as well. Being part of the mission of church is written into who we are. When we lose touch with that we lose touch with a hugely important source of our own happiness and well-being.

My hope is based on what I think are two really positive signs. Firstly, there is a widespread openness to the gospel in our society despite many of the negative currents in that society. Secondly, those of us who experience the call to reach out with the good news already have the capacity to do so. In the coming pages I want to offer what I think are good reasons for holding these two positions. I also want to explore two central implications for us as church if we are to positively respond to these signs:

1 To move closer to the people of our time, especially those on the edge of church and society. To bring an open heart and a listening ear so that we can become better attuned to the hopes and struggles of their lives and learn how to offer the gospel as a gift to those lives.
2 To move beyond a model of leadership that limits discernment and decision making on key pastoral issues to male clerics. We have the capacity to effectively mission in today's society if we fully draw on the energy, the imagination and the experience of women and men, lay and cleric.

A troubled spirit
The hope that can give us momentum into the future is not based on a naïve, other-worldly spirituality. It is not blind to negative signs in both church and society. Certainly that hope is not overwhelmed by the negative, but it does face it. It seeks to draw lessons from it.

It is not possible in these times to write about the church in Ireland without reference to clerical child abuse and how church authorities have handled it. What kind of sign is that for us? What is it calling us to? I find myself along with so many others hugely troubled by these questions. It is very hard to get a clear perspective on this when we are in the middle of it but my gut sense is that we are called to a conversion that is about more than putting in place adequate structures and procedures to ensure the protection of children. I think the issue points to something fundamentally wrong in how we are as church, something that infects all of our life and mission. I think this enormously destructive, negative sign is calling us precisely to the same place as the positive signs – to a mission based on listening to the people and to shared leadership.

In a statement following publication of the Ferns report (25 October 2005) Archbishop Diarmuid Martin described as 'unforgivable' the fact that those who had knowledge of child abuse did not act on it. The failure of leadership that this refers to was not an isolated incident. It had been normal practice; it was systemic. This raises a whole host of questions: What were the factors that conditioned the response of the church leadership over the last number of decades to the issue of child abuse? What caused such a widespread failure of human imagination and empathy? What was it about their formation in theology and spirituality that allowed this to happen? What was it about the structures of decision making that left their own malpractice so long unchallenged? What was it about the nature of their relationship with the Vatican that brought them to pay more attention to religious bureaucratic issues than to their own people? What was it about the routine practices of their lives – whom they met with, listened to, deemed worthy of attention – that left them out of touch with reality? And to what extent are these factors still present and impacting on other areas of church life?

I am conscious that these are painful questions at a time when the present leadership is already hurting deeply. But this is not a personal issue; it is not about scapegoating individuals. I believe that if I had been formed in the same manner and put in the same role as they, I would have behaved no differently. I don't make this point flippantly; for me it is a deadly serious admission, one that highlights the fact that this is an issue about a church system that conditions us all, perhaps especially those who achieve leadership within it.

Here I will use the metaphor of the body. If a body is otherwise normal and healthy it will register if something has gone wrong in some part of it. It will feel the pain and be moved to take action. If the body does not react in that way it has more wrong with it than the diseased part. Some fundamental bodily sensitivity is missing or not properly functioning. Child abuse is like a diseased hand in the body of the church. It should have been a source of unbearable pain. But it wasn't. Whatever way the head or brain was functioning it was able to accommodate the disease, to hide it. It didn't seem to be able to feel the pain enough. Now that the diseased hand has been exposed there is a great rush to have it amputated, as if to say the problem is only in the hand and once we get rid of that there will be no other problem. I do not see at all the same rush to even recognise, still less attend to, the malfunctioning of the whole body.

The issue of child abuse is a sign and symptom of a wider illness in the church body. Of itself, amputating the hand that has offended will not deal with this illness. The illness will only re-manifest itself. Now instead of hiding the diseased hand, insensitive to the pain of victims, we will chop off every accused finger, but we will still be insensitive to the pain caused; still likely to make terrible mistakes in this and other areas of church life.

There is so much positive for us as church to do and be in this new society of ours. There is a mission we have to move on to, but not without attending to our illness. I do not know how we can do this but I think it starts in the heart – in repentance and conversion. It starts in a recognition – and I think this burden falls especially but not exclusively on leadership – that there is something wrong in how we have been and in how we are. This is what repentance is about: recognising and then exploring the nature and causes of our systemic illness. This is not about wallowing in the negative; it is about dealing with the problem so that we can be free and competent to move on.

I do not for a minute doubt the good will of our present leadership, but I believe that our credibility as church is greatly compromised if we do not have a deep and honest inquiry into these questions. Any talk of atonement will ring hollow without such an inquiry. It is not only issues to do with child protection that are at stake here. If there is a systemic flaw that has left us dysfunctional in this area how can we know that we are not dysfunctional in other areas as well? What about our primary task of evangelisation? I think it is reasonable to at least raise the question of whether the systems that caused such a momentous failure of the imagination when it came to protecting children will not equally cause a failure of the imagination when it comes to effectively communicating the gospel in contemporary culture. These are complex, energy-demanding issues at a time when morale is low, particularly among the clergy, and especially at leadership level. Who has the heart to even begin to explore them? What is striking at present in regard to child protection is the extent to which exploration of key questions and decision making has moved away from an exclusively clerical milieu. The national audit is a dramatic example of this and represents a deeply interesting sign of the times – the wider society calling church systems to accountability on a fundamental moral issue.

If repentance is about recognising our systemic illness, conversion is about a resultant change of practice. I believe that one fundamental implication for leadership practice is simple: *we cannot handle this on our own; we need the help and wisdom and experience of others*. In the case of child protection the burden of responsibility has been lifted, indeed taken from, church leadership. There is a wider structure within which they are now being made accountable. But for the other questions there is no such structure. No external body is going to initiate an inquiry into the church if we are negligent in regard to evangelisation. We have to create our own space to address this and other challenges. My own sense is that for us to do that in a way that is faithful to our gospel mandate there needs to be a leap now in terms of our leadership structures at all levels of the Irish church. A leap away from an exclusively male, clerical milieu for reflection and decision making on major issues to one that includes laity and religious, women and men. This is already happening to an extent at parish level with parish pastoral councils becoming the norm rather than the exception. However, it needs to happen at diocesan and national level as well. Just as clergy are no longer responding on their own to the challenges of child protection neither should they be responding on their own to other major challenges facing the church.

Pastoral councils are urgently needed now, at all levels, as places of discernment, energy and hope for the future of our mission as church; as *the* places where the key pastoral questions are addressed. Councils made up of people with the capacity and commitment for this, who care passionately about the mission of the church in our country but are not yes-men and yes-women. There are plenty of such people available in our parishes; people who have the life experience that can help them to understand and connect with the life experiences of the wider community; people who are at the coalface of the culture in terms of their family life, their neighbourhood, their workplace; people who are in a position to listen deeply to the hurts and hopes of the culture and begin to construct effective ways of bringing the good news of the gospel to bear on these.

I am not dismissing the life-experience of celibate clergy and religious. I know many personally and have immense regard for their graceful humanity, for their ongoing generosity and self-giving, for their commitment to an ideal. Theirs is overwhelmingly an extraordinary gift to our church and to our culture. But I think it is a gift that would be immensely more valuable in a different kind of church. There is something about how we are organised as church that is choking our potential. Our system of leadership restricted to male clergy and (predominantly male) religious is part of the problem. That system needs to be broken open.

I find this whole question of internal church structures troubling and de-energising. Our mission is to reach out. Our structures are only at the service of this mission. Overly focusing on structures means that we are taking our eye off the ball. For many years my sense has been to get on with the mission and to leave the structures to sort themselves out. The child abuse issue has moved me on this. It has brought me to the conviction that in order to be faithful to our mission we need to also challenge our structures.

CHAPTER

3 Down in the valley

My home is on an acre of garden. This garden always felt very big and complicated when I was stuck into some specific piece of work – digging the vegetable patch, cleaning out the chicken run, laying paths and planting shrubs in the grassed area. One day a man arrived at my door with a photograph of the garden that he had taken from an aeroplane. I was delighted and hugely comforted by it: for the first time I had a perspective on my garden. I could hold it all in a single view, see its smallness in the context of the bog land all around, see its shape. See much more clearly the possibilities of making the garden into what I longed for – a simple and beautiful space. Most importantly for me, I could see the key tasks that needed to be done to achieve this. Once I had this bigger picture I got new energy and new focus for my gardening work.

As a pastoral worker in the garden of the Irish church I would dearly love a photograph like that. I feel most of the time that my nose is stuck into particular tasks that seem big and complicated, and I cannot feel sure that where I am putting my energy or what I am doing with it is what is needed. I would love to be able to see clearly the patterns in what is happening here and now, to see the possibilities, the key tasks that would realise these possibilities. What I want to see most is this: where God is walking the garden; where God has already tilled and planted. I know that there is much that is damaging the garden – cultural pollution, big church trees blocking the light and so on. But I know too in my heart that something powerfully positive and beautiful is happening here now under my nose; something obvious, though I cannot see it clearly. My nightmare is that I will live long enough to read the first histories of this turn-of-century Irish church. The historians will fly over the ground we have walked on and effortlessly photograph the patterns we missed, the opportunities we could not see.

Of course, we do not have an aeroplane; there is nobody yet to fly over this time and place. We are all on the ground, in our different patches. However, that does not mean we cannot get some perspective, especially if we can swap stories, and struggle to imagine the patterns that make sense of our stories, that can help us to discern and take heart from the signposts of God's presence among us. I have had opportunities to be with and listen to the stories of many people working hard in pastoral ministry. I will offer an image that stays with me from those stories:

Not a garden this time, but a valley. We in ministry are like refugees in a new country, limping down to the bottom of a cold, dark valley. Behind us a long slope of decline in our sense of pastoral effectiveness in the new country and ahead of us a mountain of unanswered pastoral questions. There are many tracks up this mountain, but we are used to the level, well-beaten paths of the old country. We are tired and have not much energy for a messy, uncertain climb.

Why do we not have much energy? I found the following diagram helpful in looking at this question. What it tries to get at is simple enough: some of us in the church are very comfortable with religious questions – we enjoy studying, exploring ideas and possibilities; others are happier being involved in hands-on, practical ways – we love to apply religious answers. If these different approaches are put on a scale we get something such as below.

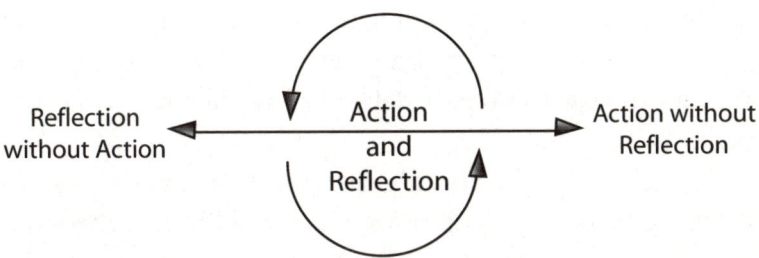

On one extreme of the scale there is an emphasis on reflection, on exploring pastoral questions, but without much pastoral action; on the other end of the scale there is a lot emphasis on pastoral action, on delivery, on working with answers but little by way of exploring questions. At the centre there is the emphasis on both action and reflection, with the action feeding the reflection, and the reflection in turn feeding further action.

In my experience most of us involved in ministry are more comfortable at the action end of the scale. We like action, delivery, working with definite tasks. While all is going well with our tasks there is no problem for us. However, we go into crisis when what we are doing no longer works. That leaves us stuck. The only place we can move to is back towards exploring questions. Generally, we will only go there as a last resort.

The point I want to emphasise here is that this is not surprising. Most of us were formed in a church that valued answers more than questions, that offered us answers even when we did not have questions. We find it hard to shift from there to a situation where we have questions without ready answers, yet that is precisely the challenge that faces us: to learn through trial and error, through action and reflection, how to be pastorally effective in a new time and place.

While the gospel doesn't change, the means we use to offer the gospel as gift must change with the changing circumstances. Pope John Paul makes this point clearly: 'The programme…is the same as ever. Ultimately it has its centre in Christ himself, who is to be known, loved and imitated...' However, he goes on to say that the work of spreading the gospel 'must be translated into pastoral initiatives adapted to the circumstances of each community' *(At the Beginning of the New Millennium,* n. 29).

This is not just the conviction of the Pope; I believe it is also part of the *sensus fidelium,* the common sense of the people of God. This came through to me very powerfully from my involvement in a number of diocesan consultations in preparation for pastoral plans. The consultations sought to hear the burning issues of the people and their hopes for the church. What follows is a brief summary of the key patterns coming from one such consultation (Killaloe diocese), patterns that are typical of consultations across the country.

Connecting with our life struggles

The people consulted are hoping for a church that can connect with their lives, speak to and be relevant to their concerns. The underlying intuition here is that the good news is not a disembodied, disconnected piece of information that is the same for all people in all circumstances.

Connecting with people on the margins

While concern for people on the margins of society is not the dominant issue it is strongly present. Among the people involved in church ministry there was a social sense expressed in terms of unhappiness about the decline in community and spiritual values in society, especially in regard to justice for people on the margins. This sense also came through in some of the young parent groups. A strong moral sensibility was expressed here in terms of concerns about corruption, injustice and violence in society. There was also a concern about the pace of life and its impact, particularly on the young. The hope was that the church could be an agent for building community, a voice for people who are hurting in our society.

The strongest hopes in this regard were expressed by groups of people on the margins, for example the elderly and refugees. The strong feelings among the elderly were to do with loneliness and fear – days may go by without any human contact and there is fear of being attacked, or of becoming ill and dying alone. Hopes for the church centred on it speaking out for the elderly and being an agent for developing caring activities in the communities to meet the needs of the elderly. For the refugees their hopes for the church centred on it being a centre of support for refugees as a marginal community – befriending them, providing information, speaking out on their behalf and providing them with opportunities for involvement in church life and liturgy.

Caring for people in ministry

The underlying thrust of the above is its sense that the gospel treasures and is sensitive to human experience. This sense comes out in another way in the consultations – in the need to care for not only the people ministered to, but also the people ministering. There is a strong message here: pay attention to the experience of priests and people involved in ministry; do not take them for granted; put energy and resources into their formation and ongoing support.

Having a missionary spirit

This vision element was expressed explicitly by involved laity. Their hope for the church was that it would be a more vibrant, vital presence in society, listening to and engaged with people's concerns, more effectively able to offer the good news of the gospel, more inclusive. They want church to be more confident about what we have to offer the culture. They want church to have the heart and the energy to get up and get out there with its good news. Overall the mood was quite positive and at times people were impatient for developments to happen. There was a strong sense throughout that as a church we are not nearly achieving our potential. We need to communicate better our good news with the culture at large. We need to utilise far more our latent talents and energy. This hope for a missionary church is present in a more implicit way in the focus groups among the general population. Here it is expressed in terms of a church that can reach out to them and to their children.

Having a missionary footing

We need to shift from a pastoral strategy of maintenance to one of mission. This hope is expressed strongly in the groups. The basic sense here is that our pastoral structures need to be at the service of a missionary outreach. Unfortunately, the structures we have inherited do not suffice for this. A number of elements are included in this:

- Having a clear set of pastoral priorities for our current situation and a pastoral strategy for their implementation
- Fostering a greater involvement of lay people in planning, making decisions on and implementing pastoral priorities
- Supporting and resourcing of lay people for this
- Supporting and forming priests for the missionary challenge and for working with lay people
- Providing people with expertise to offer a back-up service for key parish ministries
- Putting in place structures at diocesan and cluster levels to manage the implementation of the pastoral priorities, particularly in view of the declining numbers of priests
- Putting the material resources of the diocese at the service of its missionary outreach.

How are dioceses responding? The pastoral sense across the country is broadly the same – a recognition of a new cultural context putting the old pastoral systems under pressure and a need for some form of planned pastoral response. The core concerns are to do with managing the pastoral workload in a more collaborative way (with reduced numbers of priests and religious) and at the same time responding to the need to reach out in some way to those who have disconnected from church.

While the decline in church practice is a key concern, there is also a concern about the many pressures that the new cultural situation is putting on individuals, families and communities, both among the affluent and the poor.

This situation creates a hugely difficult dilemma for many church people. On the one hand, they have a strong sense that the good news of the gospel is more relevant than ever. On the other hand, they have a frustrating sense of not knowing how to respond, of not feeling equipped to offer the gospel as gift to this new culture. Across the country pastoral planning is marked by a sense of hope that the church in Ireland can be an effective agent of the gospel today, but also by a deep sense of fragility. Many pastoral people experience themselves in the valley-type situation mentioned above. This is a very difficult place for them to be in and can result in a kind of pastoral semi-paralysis, characterised by hesitant movement, partial movement or even resistance to movement.

Across the country many efforts at pastoral planning have a stop–go dynamic. Questions are explored, decisions are taken and some of the decisions are followed up; others are not, however. The questions are then returned to again, sometimes with a demoralising sense that 'we have been here before'. Among many there is a sense that a pre-condition for a new movement 'up the mountain of questions' is a movement 'in', towards deeper spirituality, stronger fraternity and greater personal care for people in ministry. Without this inner movement there may be little energy for the movement 'out' and 'up'.

There are a number of features common to all the diocesan responses:

- A missionary dimension – a desire to reach out and connect with those who are on the margins of church and society

- A spiritual dimension – a desire to deepen through liturgy, prayer and catechesis the faith life of those involved in church
- A collaborative dimension – a desire to create partnerships among priests, religious and laity in carrying through on the above work
- Care for priests – a recognition of the need for a culture of solidarity among priests, for systems of good practice in the care for, formation of and employment of priests
- A difficulty with change – while there is a recognition of the need for change and a desire for change, the actual practice of change comes hard.

So how will things work out? If one of the images that future generations will have of us is a church people descending into a valley, what other images might they have? Will there be images of us nurturing and gathering around the fires of our faith, offering warmth and friendship to one another in our difficult time? Will there be images of us lighting torches from those fires and gently, in good humour, exploring the tracks that will take us out of the valley up the side of the mountain? Will there be images of us discovering in time the best tracks, the plateaus along the way that will mark our progress step by step?

One thing I am sure of: there are tracks available to us up the mountain that can take us into a new place of pastoral effectiveness. There are plateaus that offer realistic shorter-term destinations in what may be a long climb. The only thing to fear is that we will lose heart in this valley time; that future pictures will show us dissipating our energies, grumbling, scattering, huddling for what isolated comfort we can find; staying put and dying where we are. Not a pretty picture! And, of course, not inevitable.

One of the things that can free us to move is simply to recognise why we find it difficult to move – and not to panic about it. To have a sense of faith and trust that if God is calling us to mission, God recognises and accepts us for who we are and where we are. God has a sense of humour! God will give us what we need as we move. There is an old prayer that might have a new resonance for us at this time; one that might help us on our journey:

> The Lord is my Shepherd, there is nothing I shall want...
> Though I walk in the valley of darkness
> you are there with your rod and your staff to guide me.

CHAPTER 4
'Find the traces of the Spirit'

I remember a night some years ago when I was part of an invited audience to a special *Late Late Show* on the state of the church in Ireland. There were many people I knew from different parts of the country – all of us there because we were in some way involved in church. Before the show started we were gathered in a reception area, standing around chatting in groups with pre-show drinks. In my group there was a hugely animated discussion and much laughter. What were we talking about? Not the state of the church for sure. We were wondering what there was going to be for everyone in the audience!

Then a few minutes before we moved into the studio one of the programme staff stood up on a box in the middle of the floor and called our attention. 'Because of the kind of show we are having tonight,' she announced, 'because of its serious nature, we won't be having anything for everyone in the audience.' I felt a bit deflated at first and then angry. I wondered, what kind of people does she think we are? Does she not think that church people want to have a bit of fun the same as everyone else?

Is there something out of place about having a light diversion in the middle of a religious conversation? After a while I calmed down and began to think again. Maybe it is not her I should be blaming at all. Maybe there is something about us church people that gives the impression that we are somehow very staid and serious; that we cannot or do not enjoy ourselves.

Wouldn't that be odd? A group of people claiming to have some very good news, yet looking anything but happy! However, I think there is some truth in it. This is how we are, at least sometimes. I remember vividly coming home from a parish gathering one night, my spirits a bit flattened. The purpose of the gathering had been to look at possible developments in parish ministry. The mood had been very negative. One of the participants summarised that negativity powerfully and simply: 'When I was young,' he said, 'things were good in this parish.' They are bad now, and they're going to get worse!

Not surprisingly there was no outcome from the meeting. There was a sense of despondency about the younger generations; a sense of anger towards them for having abandoned what the gathering regarded as precious; a sense of wanting to abandon them in turn. There was no life, no hope, no energy there. Yet these were people who did care about church, who had been touched by faith, who wanted to see faith and church alive and well. So what had happened to them? What way of thinking had they become locked into that paralysed their energy?

I am not trying to single out this gathering of people. I want to raise a question for all of us because I think we can all be like that at least some of the time – I know I certainly was. For me the reason for thinking and feeling that way was simple enough. It was to do with the fundamental way I had come to see the world and God in the world.

As a teenager I got involved in a Catholic group that did evangelisation work with young people. We simply stopped them as they were walking up and down the street and asked if we could talk to them about God. One in ten or twenty would stop and engage with us and there were many interesting conversations. However, what I remember most vividly are the meetings we used to have in preparation for the street work. The basic message given to us at these meetings was that we were doing God's work in a world gone to hell. We were like God's army stealing into the devil's territory. God was in us and our responsibility was to allow God to work through us to rescue as many souls as possible.

There were two things especially that I took on board from this. Firstly, that God was not in the world out there; he was in me and in those with me, against the world. With that perspective I was inclined to be tense, intense and intolerant in how I worked. I also had an abiding sense of being burdened by a task too big. I felt angry and resentful towards all those who were not like me.

Secondly, what I took in was that *it was down to me*. God was dependent on me and required me to reach a very high level of holiness if I were not to fail him. While at the start this was exhilarating and left me with an abiding sense of vocation, after a while it began to wear me down. I could not reach the spiritual standard required and felt a failure before God. This was a hugely discouraging and de-energising experience for me.

Had I stayed that way I know I could not have long sustained my involvement. I moved on to other involvements and was blessed to come into contact with many people who worked from a very different spirituality. Over time they changed me. A key moment for me in this was a meeting with a priest who was offering me a job in the midlands. I was not able to quite grasp what he was looking for and asked him to summarise the job for me. His exact words were: 'Find the traces of the Spirit and follow them.'

It took a while but the significance of his words gradually dawned on me and unburdened my heart in a fundamental way. He was saying to me that God is already out there ahead of me working in the world. It is God's territory I am going in to, not the devil's. It is not all down to me, but I can help, I can cooperate. He was also saying *Look out for signs of God's work*. This did not mean to be naïve about the power of negative forces in the world, but to have a nose for and a firm grasp on the positive in the midst of the negative. To explore the possibilities that are offered through what is good out there.

So, is the world out there a spiritual and moral desert or is it a place where God's spirit is active? I believe it is the latter. In his book *New Life for Old* (2004) Fr Vincent McNamara offers a perspective on this question. He develops a clear and inspiring vision for ministry based on what people actually desire (rather than what we think they ought to desire!). I am hugely touched by his calm, gentle, compassionate analysis. It strikes me as so real and yet so encouraging. He recognises chaos, confusion and internal contradiction in our desires, but also the presence of a depth that is moral and open to the transcendent; a depth which means that faith and morality cannot be viewed as external impositions on people, but as responses to desires already there.

I find this point crucial when it comes to the question of energy for ministry in today's culture. Many of us harbour doubts about whether people are open to what we have to offer. We have a sense of ourselves seeking to impose on them what they do not want. But McNamara is quietly insistent that people are drawn to the good, the true and the beautiful. These are core elements in our deepest desires for full human becoming. 'We are...a vast polyphony of desires. Within them is a richly sonorous moral strand. It is among our deepest instincts. It is our natural sense that there is a way of being with others that is intelligent, that is meaningful, that is our flourishing. It enshrines the transpersonal qualities of goodness, generosity, forgiveness and love. It is our soul-life. Genuine moral life is about listening to that, allowing it more space, more influence in our daily lives, allowing it to exercise its gentle attraction over us' (p. 70).

McNamara recognises why it is not easy for us to be in touch with this part of ourselves. Our human condition dictates that most of our energy and attention is given to basic self-referential desires such as survival, control of our environment, being loved and being esteemed. How we go about meeting these desires is itself hugely conditioned (and almost inevitably distorted) by the givens of evolution, genetics and the particulars of our childhood: 'It is not easy becoming a human being...and the child has to do it in a world where adults spend much of their time coping with their own inadequacies.' He recognises too that many features of modern society make this all the more difficult. However, far from condemning us for our failures along the way he says, 'We have done well to have survived, to be as sane as we are. We need to give full weight to the extraordinary perilous journey of human becoming...to recognise that it would have been difficult for us to be otherwise than we were' (p. 90).

Our basic ego-desires do not represent a false self to be gotten rid of; they are part of our make-up as human beings; they need to be graciously integrated into our lives in a way that they are not all-controlling, in a way that allows us to notice and attend to the deeper desires as well. There is a here a very beautiful, deeply respectful vision of the human: 'Whatever about the scars of life, in my core I am whole and precious – if only I could have a sense of that and trust it' (p. 40).

The natural openness to the transcendent is not in itself religious faith, but it brings us into the territory of faith and 'needs to be awakened before the teaching of Christ can be truly take flesh in us'. Here McNamara develops a point that is vividly critical of church:

> An increasing number of people call themselves spiritual, but are at pains to reject organised religion, in part at least because they do not recognise it as speaking to their spirit... Doctrine has been transmitted – tundras of

> cold, frozen language – that ignores the human awakening of people. (p. 57)

This is deeply encouraging in its implication that a different approach to our mission could be very fruitful. What kind of approach? One rooted in and respectful of the desire for human wholeness? One that recognises and accepts the responsibility and capacity of each individual to walk the way of wholeness? McNamara summarises this way as self-presence: 'an inner aliveness to the actuality of ourselves and to the call of our soul…a compassionate awareness both of our patterns and our possibilities' (p. 57).

As church we can support people on this journey to the heart of their desires and aspirations 'and seek to find a resonance with them in word and sacrament'. In this context his vision for liturgy is one that I find hugely inspiring and suggestive:

> Is [liturgy] not meant, above all, to be a meditative opening of our consciousness to the infinite mystery that silently envelops our lives, a link between our deepest desires and their ultimate source? (p. 57)

Likewise his vision for sacraments:

> Sacraments are to brood over the great moments of life…They are meant to speak to experience. They are a response to a desiring.

'FIND THE TRACES OF THE SPIRIT'

> If there is not an invitation into the spaces of the spirit...there is only formalism. Religion then will be impersonal, a layer of dogma and morals laid on us, but not reaching into our hearts...And so an optional extra, rather than something unquenchably of the human condition. (p. 60)

The over-riding message throughout the book, one that I find foundational for my own approach to ministry, is that each person has depth; each person has soul. In the circumstances of modern society it is especially difficult for people to be in tune with their own depth. I think the challenge for us in ministry is never to lose faith in this. There remains a depth in people that can resonate with the depth of the gospel. It may be buried deep, like gold in the mountains, but it is there!

CHAPTER

5 Travellers together

As a person involved in church activities, and seeking to involve others, I worked for many years with a simple, unspoken assumption: everybody should be like me! That assumption was an endless drain on my energy and it left me prone to frustration and disappointment. I was forever looking around and finding fault with people. Some of these people were involved in the church, but in programmes different to mine. They seemed to think that their programmes were more important than mine. Others were regular churchgoers, but seemed intent on keeping their distance from me, and others like me, who sought to involve them more. Some did not seem to give a hoot about anything at all to do with church or faith.

I find myself in a different space now; I have more of a sense that it is okay for people to be different; I have a sense that my task is not to make people become like me at all but to find the good in where they are and start with that. I find this an easier, more enjoyable space to work from. It has also made a big practical difference to how I work.

I found the following image helpful in expressing this sense. It tries to capture in a simple way the pattern of church involvement that I think is generally true in parishes.

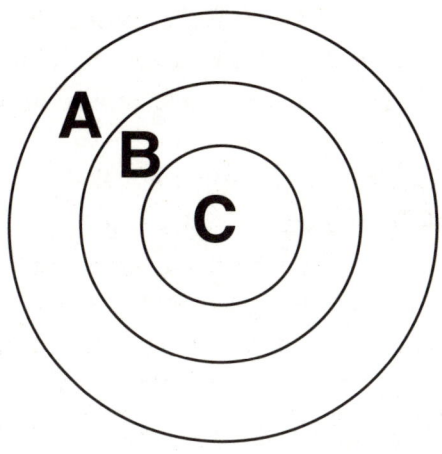

This image represents the parish within which there are broadly three groups of people. In the centre are the 'C's, who are very involved in the parish. They join groups, attend meetings and take responsibility for a great variety of parish activities. Then there are the 'B's, who are in regular contact with the parish, especially through weekend mass attendance. They are interested in, friendly towards and financially supportive of the parish but they don't want to be 'C's! On the outside are the 'A's, who are in *irregular* contact with the parish. They do not normally go to mass at the weekends and, generally, are not very interested in or engaged by what goes on in the parish. However, they do visit the church occasionally for gatherings such as weddings, funerals, baptisms, confirmations, Christmas and so on.

These three groups are not fixed; people move back and forth – 'A's become 'B's, 'B's become 'C's and *vice versa*. There is also the possibility of a complete disconnection from parish – of people moving outside the 'A' group, but this is very rare. Even among those who are ideologically non-church, how many would refuse to attend the wedding or funeral of a friend because it was in a church?

I am conscious too that with the welcome increase in the numbers of immigrants we have a greater diversity of religious faiths, including non-Christian faiths. But it remains the case that the great majority of people are baptised and have some connection with parish – some committed activists, some regular attenders, some irregular attenders. The percentage of people in the different groups varies greatly across the country. In some parishes 95 per cent of the population belong to the 'A' group; in other parishes the majority are in the 'B' and 'C' groups.

Most of us who are involved in parish activities judge the success of these activities in simple terms – how many 'B's became 'C's and how many 'A's became 'B's? The more we can get people to move towards the centre (to be like us!) the more successful we feel. And if our efforts do not produce that outcome we feel a failure. That was my view for a long time but something happened to me a few years ago that caused me to think again. I was part of a parish group preparing for a Novena to St Therese. This was in the wake of the visit of the relics of St Therese to Ireland. Our group was powerfully struck at the huge numbers that visited the relics across the country – not just the 'C's and the 'B's, but also the 'A's. So we decided to set up an annual Novena to St Therese in the parish. As part of the publicity we looked for and received permission to set up a novena information stand in the main shopping centre in the town.

As we were preparing the stand one of the group suggested that we include a prayer petition box. There was some doubt expressed that people out busy with their shopping would stop to write prayers, especially in the middle of a public space. However, we went ahead with the petition box and each day for about ten days before the novena the box was stuffed with prayer petitions. Each day we emptied the box there were hundreds and hundreds of prayer petitions, from people young and old.

We were going to have to sift through the prayers to take a selection to be read out during the novena sessions. But it struck us that it would be valuable to read them all – to get an insight into what it is that people pray about in the middle of a busy shopping centre. I read every one of them and it was one of the most powerful experiences of spiritual reading in my life. The first thing that stood out for me was the very strong, uncomplicated sense of faith coming through: 100 per cent of the petitions were prayers *of* faith. The next thing that struck me was that only about 5 per cent of the petitions were prayers *about* faith. By this I mean only a small percentage were prayers for greater faith or prayers for family members to return to church and so on. Prayers about day-to-day life made up 95 per cent of the petitions – prayers about sickness, family problems, relationships, hopes for the future. The people were praying to St Therese and to God for help in their struggles to get on with their lives.

I found myself deeply touched and disturbed by the prayers, disturbed in the positive sense that they were causing something to shift inside me. There was a significant message here for me and I struggled to see it. And then it just dawned on me: all my life I have been focused on my faith, preoccupied with my religion. I have sought to build a religion-centred life for myself. I have sought to encourage others towards a similar life and I have been despondent that so few seemed interested. What the prayers in the shopping centre taught me was that while I was right in one respect – the majority of people are not interested in a religion-centred life – what I had failed to appreciate was that they are interested in a *life-centred religion*!

For me this was a revelation, a happy revelation. It seemed obvious that there is something completely healthy and normal about people wanting to get on with the business of living the lives that God has given them. There is something very beautiful in their desire for God to accompany them in their lives, to be with them especially in moments of struggle. But where did that leave me and people like me; those whose religious sense has intruded much more into our lives so that it has become a focus of our lives? If the other people are normal does that mean we are not? Does that mean that we should try to be like them?

I want to explore these questions further, but the basic sense that I am coming to is this: difference is okay – there are many of us whose religious sense is different from the norm. The challenge for us is to be who we are, to appreciate and to enjoy who we are, but also to appreciate and enjoy others who are different. We must offer our gifts as best we can but without the precondition that everyone should be like us. I have found something hugely liberating in that perspective.

CHAPTER

6 The Spirit among the 'A's

Looking at this division of parishioners into three broad groups the main issue concerning most parishes is the growth of the 'A's. We look at all the new housing estates populated by young couples that do not come to church; we look at the great numbers of teenagers that do not come. Recent studies show that roughly three-quarters of those between 18 and 30 are now 'A's compared to only one-tenth of the over-60s.

So, how do we church people view this and how does this view shape our response? Can we spot any traces of the Spirit in the 'A' territory? Have we seen anything that gives us a realistic sense of hope that what we have to offer can be experienced as good news there? That it can evoke a positive response there?

It seems to me that we have two very different, even contradictory ways of looking at the 'A's. When we speak about them *in general* we are inclined to be critical and pessimistic, more conscious of the absence rather than the presence of the Spirit among them. Our broad explanation of the growth of the 'A's is that the materialism of modern society has deadened their moral and spiritual sensibility and so has turned them away from the gospel vision of life offered by the church. The implication here, of course, in terms of a response is that *they* are the ones that need to change while we church people hold our position

However, the 'A's are not strangers to us; they are our friends and neighbours; they are our family members. When we speak about the 'A's *who we know* we are inclined to be much more positive; we have a much stronger feel for the traces of the Spirit among them. Often I have heard 'C's taking about the young 'A's in their parishes, saying things such as, 'They don't go to Mass but they are very good'. I have also heard parents who are very committed church people speak about their children who no longer go to church. Almost always they will affirm that their children continue to have a religious and moral sense. This raises a very interesting question: if it is true that many people with moral and religious sensibility have disconnected from the church, why has that happened? Is there something about us as church people that we need to look at?

Here I want to take a closer look at the 'A's, in order to try to answer this question. What I want to highlight is that our positive sense of the 'A's has good foundation. We know all about the pressures that people are under in modern life – we know about drink, drugs, greed, violence and so on. We know how powerful consumerism is and how shallow a vision it has for human living. One historian of civilisation, Fr Thomas Berry, says that consumerism offers the narrowest vision of human life since humankind emerged from the Stone Age! This makes for a very cramped space for something as deep and as wide as the gospel.

So we know that the false gods of wealth and greed are powerful. But what I want to highlight here is that they are *not all-powerful.* Among those who have disconnected from church there continue to flow very strong currents of religious and moral sensibility. There is a depth among the 'A's in tune with the depth of the gospel. For me that is certainly a trace of the Spirit that is worth following.

For example, a national study (European Values Survey 1999) shows that only 1 per cent of the population as a whole say they are convinced atheists; over 90 per cent of people pray; over 90 per cent of people go to church at least on occasion; over 90 per cent of people believe it important to have religious ceremonies at key moments in their lives – births, marriages and deaths. Taking out all the 'B's and 'C's from these figures this still means that the majority of the 'A's continue to believe in God, pray to God and go to church occasionally.

Another recent study shows a very strong religious sense among young people with third-level education (Dr Des O'Donnell, *Doctrine and Life*, January 2001). These people are mainly in the 'A' territory. Only 4 per cent say that God has no influence on their lives; only 6 per cent deny or do not care about life after death. The words they used most to describe their experience of God were 'peace', 'trust', 'love' and 'joy'. Only 2 per cent of females and 11 per cent of males say they never pray; only 14 per cent of males, 5 per cent of females and 1 per cent of young married *never* go to mass.

THE SPIRIT AMONG THE 'A's

My point here is not to suggest that everything is really fine regarding the religious sense of the 'A's. Certainly, in moving out from the circle of 'B's (those who engage regularly in public worship) they have made a major religious shift. However, it is not a shift in the main to irreligion. It is more a shift towards an informal and private religion. Their religious sense has not gone away. I think it is absolutely crucial that we do not lose sight of this fact. There is something very substantial to work with and to build on.

So what about the moral sense of the 'A's? Let's look again at the O'Donnell survey on young adults. His conclusion is that his research shows no evidence that the young people live by an *à la carte* morality. He finds a consistency of moral position among all the groups of young people he surveyed. He offers a list of the behaviours that the young find most immoral. At the top of the list comes sexual abuse of children, followed by physical abuse in marriage, verbal abuse in marriage, abortion for reasons of convenience and taking from another's rights and freedoms. Church positions on sexual morality such as cohabitation and contraception come lowest on the list.

In the young people's hopes for their future children, what comes across strongly is a feel for the whole development of the child, a concern for the child's spirit, with personal development, personal well-being and having good relationships being rated more highly than material success and comfort. A similar broad moral sense is evident in the population as a whole. In the European Values study 95 per cent of people would like to see greater emphasis on family in the future; 82 per cent would like to have a simpler and more natural lifestyle; and 69 per cent would like to see less emphasis on money.

So in the light of all this I think it is too simple to say that the reason people have moved away from the church is that their hearts have been hardened by materialism and secularism; that they are no longer open to the things of the Spirit. This is not to deny that there is some truth in that perspective. It is certainly true that the church has tried to keep before society a sense of God within us and within our neighbour. As a quiet voice for the spiritual in life it has sometimes been drowned out by the loud music of entertainment, the shrill voice of the advertisers. However, this is not the whole picture. It is not simply a question of what is positive in the church being overwhelmed by what is negative in society. I believe that what is positive about modern society has exposed what is negative about the church.

What do I mean by this? Irish society has modernised very quickly in recent decades. Everywhere it happens modernisation powerfully affects how people see themselves and how they see the world. One of the ways it does this is that it creates a much higher sense of the individual. Personal choice, personal freedom and personal experience come to be much more emphasised. Fr Pat Collins summarises this very well. He talks about 'a shift from the experience of authority to the authority of experience'. In our more traditional-type society there was much more experience of authority and fear of authority – we feared our parents, our teachers, our bosses, our priests, our God. The community we lived in was itself a kind of authority over us – it was very hard to be different and if we were different we were often treated harshly. In modern society the emphasis has shifted from authorities outside ourselves to our sense of authority within.

So while older generations were more likely to accept authoritarian type behaviour – even if they did not necessarily like it – those of us born since the 1950s are far less likely to do so. As a result, authority figures in all walks of life – teachers, parents, priests and so on – have come under pressure. My own sense is that there is something very positive about this aspect of the modern world; something that is in the spirit of the gospel. When Pope John Paul speaks about the gospel as another name for amazement at the dignity of the person, we can see the connection.

The point I am coming to is this: I believe that if we are going to be able to reconnect with the 'A's, we need to appreciate that one of the reasons they have moved away from us is precisely because of that sense of dignity. They have experienced the church as a place where their dignity was not respected. Their sense of personal freedom, personal experience and personal authority has reacted against a church system that they have experienced as autocratic and paternalistic. They have reacted against what they experienced as the imposition of a spirituality, the imposition of beliefs, practices and so on – the lack of respect for individual experience and wisdom. For many, the church has lost its credibility; it has lost its relevance. It does not speak to them in a language that touches their experience; that resonates with the hopes and the longings inside them. I think there is something very healthy in this that we need to affirm.

So, there is a challenge for us as we try to enter into dialogue with the 'A's. It genuinely does not occur to many of them that the church has anything to offer them. They have experienced a church that was given shape in a different time. The reality is that many never heard or experienced much good news from that church. This may sound very harsh and may even be offensive to some; however, I think it is the truth and I can accept this truth without feeling that I am attacking the good men and women who were part of that church.

I have found the following diagram helpful in summarising this overall picture. It distinguishes between the presence of spiritual and moral values in our society on the one hand and formal church practice on the other hand. It suggests four possible 'territories' in our society. Two we are familiar with. Territory 1 is where the church at its best is still present; where faith is lived out and celebrated; where liturgy and life come together in a way that is authentic. Territory 4 is the negative part of modern society that we frequently criticise; that is the territory that has disconnected from church and has embraced all that is worst in terms of materialism and secularism. But there are two other territories that we tend to recognise less. Territory 2 – that space in society that has disconnected from the church but that continues to hold on to spiritual and moral values to a high degree. I believe there are many 'A's in that space. And finally territory 3 – that space in the church where we have become desensitised to the moral and spiritual depths of the gospel, though we continue to preach and celebrate that same gospel. In recent years we have got a more vivid and painful sense of this space.

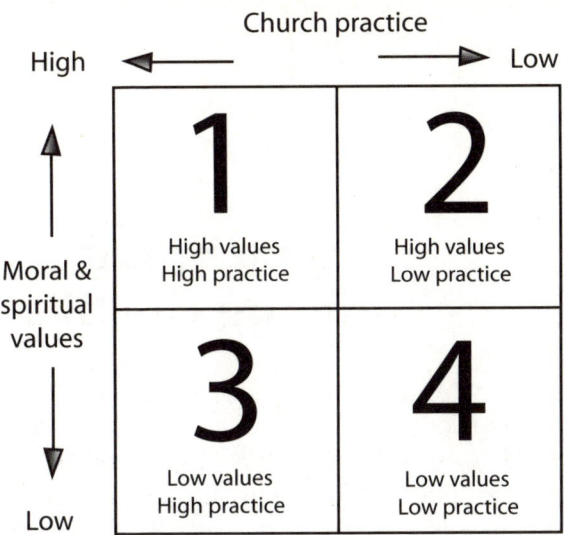

For me, the very good news from this analysis is that there is in the 'A' territory a depth that is not at all alien to the depth of the gospel. It is a depth calling us to the integrity of our own depth, calling us to fidelity to the gospel. When we think about the challenge of Pope John Paul II to go out into the deep, we are not going into wholly inhospitable territory. God's Spirit is already there ahead of us. We are calling to a depth that is already calling to us. This echoes an old and beautiful prayer:

> Why so cast down my soul, why sigh within me?
> Hope in God, I shall praise him yet,
> my saviour and my God...
> Deep is calling on deep
> in the roar of mighty waters...

CHAPTER

7   The Spirit among the 'B's

As a 'C' looking at the 'A's and 'B's, I feel called to a space where I am confident about who I am, but not arrogant; where I am grateful for the gifts I bring as a 'C', but also grateful for what the 'A's and the 'B's offer me. In this chapter I want to suggest the gift that the 'B's bring.

I have met with and worked with thousands of committed church people over the years. My impression is that sometimes we communicate a sense of hope and happiness. We seem to be enjoying our lives and our faith. But sometimes I think we come across as pessimistic, cranky and rigid; sometimes we seem to be surveying those around us from a kind of religious and moral high ground, and finding them wanting. I have been at so many meetings where I hear comments such as 'It's the same old faces!' and the underlying question is 'Where are the others?' – meaning, of course, 'Where are the 'B's?' There is something about our way of looking at our commitments that bring us to resent the people who do not share them. I think this is something we need to free ourselves from.

THE SPIRIT AMONG THE 'B's

I have always taken my religion very seriously. There is a sense in which I have taken it much too seriously. One of the things I find myself praying for now is a sense of humour, an ability to laugh at myself a little; to have a bit of fun in the ups and the downs of my journey; to see the funny side of my own perplexity in the face of the modern world; to spot the loveliness of those who are different from me; and to enjoy their conversations and their company.

A W.B. Yeats poem 'The Fiddler of Dooney' speaks to me in a delightful way on this. With a couple of marvellous images Yeats contrasts lightly and humorously the religion-centred life of the 'C's with the life-centred religion of the 'B's:

> When I play on my fiddle in Dooney,
> folk dance like a wave on the sea;
> my brother is priest in Kilvarnet,
> my cousin in Moharabuiee.
>
> I passed my brother and cousin,
> they read in their book of prayer;
> I read in my book of songs
> that I bought at the Sligo fair.

I recognise something of myself in the brother and cousin – the serious 'C's with our noses stuck in our religion books. In the fiddler and the folk who dance I see the 'B's. Now Yeats moves this scene on to heaven.

> When we come to the end of time,
> to Peter sitting in state;

> he will smile on the three old spirits,
> but call me first through the gate.
>
> For the good are always the merry,
> save by an evil chance;
> and the merry love the fiddle
> and the merry love to dance.
>
> And when the folk there spy me,
> they will all come up to me
> with 'Here is the fiddler of Dooney!'
> and dance like a wave of the sea.

There is a lovely inclusive line here – 'he will smile on the three old spirits'. From the perspective of heaven we are all okay. But it is the fiddler who is called in first! What do we 'C's make of that? It is not the ones who centred their lives on religion who get pride of place, but the ones who got on with and enjoyed their lives! And what do we make of the closing image? The folk in heaven gathered round the fiddler, delighted to see him again, and having a dance! A beautiful affirmation of a life-centred religion, with heaven offering a continuity of what the folk enjoyed most on earth.

I appreciate that the analogy I am drawing here may be offensive to some 'C's. I would have been offended myself a few years ago! However, the poem challenges a very deep religious perspective that I had long held: that at its core religion is about another life; that really religious people are more interested in the next life than this; that preoccupation with this life is somehow a slight on religion, giving it less importance than is its due and, by extension, giving religious people less importance than is their due!

Now I feel something very attractive and true in the perspective of the poem. Instead of feeling slighted when people don't share my religious preoccupation I feel now that I want to celebrate that. I have a sense that there is something fundamentally right and healthy about the 'B's approach to religion. We know better now than ever before how we human beings are part of the evolution of the universe over many of millions of years. As human life developed it was written into our genes to struggle to survive. Furthermore, because we are literally of the earth we are profoundly attached to the earth; we enjoy and long for the fruits of the earth as good in themselves.

We experience ourselves as spiritual beings and our spirits delight in the material. There is no contradiction here; that is part of our inner depth. Our spirits delight in the non-material also and, again, without contradiction. So we love things such as music, art, friendship, love, belonging, happiness and peace. Because we experience ourselves as spiritual we have always intuited a spiritual cause. Throughout human history we have had a sense of God and of wanting to relate to God. We have a sense of having an affinity with God, a sense of wanting God on our side as we struggle to get on with the task of living. We have always wondered what God is like and how we might connect with God. This is still true today in our modern world, even if it is far less obvious than before. This is saying to me that the basic orientation of our modern culture is still good in itself. People desire and are focused on living life to the full – beyond survival they want to experience the delights of life in both material and non-material ways.

Jesus continues to be profoundly relevant and attractive in our own time. Not because authority figures say so, but because people continue to have spiritual depth and spiritual questions. Two thousand years ago Jesus offered answers to these profound questions, answers that were experienced as very good news. The gift of his gospel is that it offered a vision of the delights of life in the fullest and deepest sense. It is not bad news seeking to draw people from what their hearts most desire; it is good news offering them the fullness of what they desire, offering them a sense of direction in their quest for wholeness and happiness. The good news does not point us away from the world; it points us through it and beyond it.

The way that I, and many 'C's like me, have been religiously formed had left me with a sense that religion is somehow in opposition to the fundamental thrust of the world; that bringing a religious sense to the world was like having to push a big boulder back uphill. Now I think that is a mistaken perspective. I think it is much more like running with the boulder, working with its momentum and seeking to direct that momentum with a few well-timed nudges.

CHAPTER

8   The Spirit among the 'C's

I have known many religious people over the years, people for whom faith is a central, life-long pre-occupation. Many of these work as priests and religious at home or as missionaries abroad. Others are lay people. In the context of the A and B groups the intensity of their religious convictions and commitments is unusual, but that does not mean that it is not normal. In the wide, diverse music of the Spirit they strike a beautiful, distinctive and authentically human note.

I think the challenge for religious people is to be at ease with ourselves and with others; to live and enjoy our religious sense; to share that sense without trying to impose it; to be a religious presence among others in the best, deepest sense that this means, without insisting that people be like us, without feeling superior or holier; to recognise that our religiousness is not some kind of moral quality that we can claim credit for – it is more like an artistic temperament that insists on expressing itself.

This point came home to me vividly when a woman who taught me in Junior Infants shared this story with me.

She was talking to the class about God, who made the world. She remembered me sitting in the front desk, a four year old, wide-eyed and entranced by what she was saying. I put up my hand and asked, 'Who made God?' That was all that was in her story, but it touched me greatly. I went back to it many times because I knew it was speaking something to me. What it was saying was simply this: *I have been religious all my life. I didn't choose to be. It was a given. There was something in my make up that oriented me that way from the beginning. It is part of who I am, the very same as if I were born with a gift for art or music.*

Being comfortable in my own religious skin is not something I have found easy. There have been many moments over the years when this unease expressed itself. One such moment I remember was very simple and undramatic, but it brought me to the heart of this question. I was part of a parish visitation team. It was a cold night and we were knocking at doors in a housing estate handing out copies of our parish booklet. A young man answered at one of the houses. He listened politely as I explained about the booklet, took a copy and then said, 'I'm watching a football match on television'. I felt dismissed. I tried not to show it and asked him how the match was going. I then left him to it.

I had a peculiar range of emotions as I walked away. Part of me was envious. I wanted to be like him, to be at home by my own fire, watching the match. More than that, I wanted to be free of the madness that was bringing me out to knock on doors in the first place. Why was I carrying this religious burden and he blissfully free of it?

THE SPIRIT AMONG THE 'C's

Another part of me felt hurt and angry that what I was doing was so casually dismissed. I wanted him to appreciate what I was doing, to respect and relate to the meaning of my commitment. The last thing I wanted was for that commitment to be treated as irrelevant and, worse, a nuisance.

But in the midst of my envy and anger there was another set of questions coming through. Why is it that I was so easily disturbed? Why was my sense of self-worth so dependent on the approval of this man? Why did I judge him in the light of his response to me? These questions were pushing me to get some perspective on the situation. This man had spent his day working. He was now relaxing, enjoying a football match. In the middle of that I knocked. He answered my knock, listened to my speech and accepted my offering. He was politely honest with me in expressing his desire to return to the match. Yet I wasn't satisfied with that – I wanted my moment, my presence to supersede what was going on for him.

I feel drawn now to move beyond that. Perhaps because I am fifty years of age now and do not want to spend the rest of my life ill at ease with myself. I would like to come home to myself, to enjoy the person that I am. To be that person irrespective of how others are or how others view me. There are two reflective activities that I find helpful in this. One, as I have suggested above, is simply to attend to, to remember my own story; to pull together the threads of my life; to see and accept the patterns that are there. A second is to put my own words on how I experience the call and the movement of the

Spirit within me. How have I experienced the gospel as good news? Why do I want to share that?

I am not talking here about a private religious sense, cut off from or different to the religious tradition that I belong to. What I am trying to get at is that religious communication is not simply about representing other people's religious ideas and language. At its core religion is about our experience of God. If we are to communicate that, we need to be in touch with it. We need to be able to speak about it from our hearts – not from somebody else's theology book or catechism. This does not mean that other people's stories are irrelevant to how we articulate our own. Other people's stories and the language they use help us to recognise and put a name on our own experiences. Our stories develop and clarify in a shared context. We are not just consumers of other people's religious products; we are also producers of religious insight. Together we build a tradition.

When I was younger I experienced religion in terms of a conflict between this life and the next. At best this life was a preparation for the next life, the real life. Now I experience it very differently. As a 'C' I am still very drawn to and engaged by religion but my sense has been greatly and, I think, positively changed by my encounters with many 'A's and 'B's. Here are some of the things that go to the heart of my religious convictions at this point in my life.

Offering people an authentic religious sense of their lives through our Christian story is a profoundly liberating project. Such a sense provides a framework for recognising and resisting efforts to make captive the human spirit, whether from political, economic, cultural or, for that matter, ecclesial sources. It offers a perspective on life against the horizon of what lies beyond it. It does so in a way that does not devalue life, but celebrates its grace and depth and beauty. It invites us to live life to the full.

The stamp of God is in our hearts. There, underneath the plethora of fears, desires, anxieties and insecurities lie our best, our deepest longings. Our Christian story offers us access to and resonates with this depth within us – it offers us a sense of what is really important in life and, in so doing, offers us a key to our happiness and fulfilment. It calls us to come home to ourselves, to cherish the wonderful, wonder-filled persons that we are. It calls us to extend that same gracious acceptance and love to others. Our Christian story invites us to an honouring and enjoyment of the material world as a gift of God. It names the extraordinary privilege of being in this world for the short time we have. It challenges us to care for and reach out to those who are denied in any way this unrepeatable opportunity for full, human living; to challenge the injustices that deny them their material and spiritual birthright. It also offers a sense of the presence of God within us and among us – God who calls us to his friendship and to friendship with one another (which is the heart of being church); God who yearns for us to be our best and happiest; who offers us support as we move through and seek to fully engage with life; who readily forgives us and helps us to pick up again when we do not live up to our best selves.

I would not have worded my faith convictions like this ten years ago. I suspect that in ten years from now I will be adding to and subtracting from this personal testimony. But this is okay – tracing the Spirit is not about following a prescribed road map. I am glad to share where I am now with others and to hear what others share in the belief that we can be gift to one another.

CHAPTER

9 Mission impermanent – not impossible!

Recently I came across Fr Vincent Donovan's *Christianity Rediscovered* (2005). He offers reflections on his missionary work among the Masai people in east Africa over a seventeen-year period from the 1960s. The book is a delightful read. It is deeply encouraging about the possibilities of evangelisation in culturally appropriate ways and powerfully critical of the western church's failure to see authentic possibilities for church beyond its own historically conditioned form. Over and over again I am struck by the relevance of his insights for the Irish situation, despite his African context.

His central point is that the task of the missionary is simply to preach the gospel. It is up to the people then to accept it or not. But if they accept it 'their response, whatever it might be, is the church' (p. 64). The church is not the content of the preaching – it is the response to that preaching. The core of an authentic response is very simple – belief, repentance, baptism, witness. Fr Donovan contends that how people express this response is a function of their own culture. It is their business – it is not for other cultures to impose.

He distinguishes between missionary work, which results in a local church, and pastoral work, which is about building up that church, fostering and nurturing its life and ministry. Pastoral work is always ongoing and incomplete. But missionary work has a clear beginning, middle and end over a relatively short period. You learn as best you can how to preach the gospel in a way that the culture can hear. You preach it and then allow people to make up their own minds. You baptise them if they accept your message. You move on, allowing them to develop their own church. He gives the example of Paul's three missionary journeys, which took about ten years in all, and compares this unfavourably with his own missionary context in east Africa, which then had been going on for over a century.

There is obviously a major difference between Fr Donovan's situation and ours in the west. His was a missionary context moving towards a pastoral one. Ours is a pastoral context becoming increasingly missionary. For us, pastoral and missionary challenges exist simultaneously and it is often very difficult to draw any clear line between them. The paradox that most of our missionary constituency is already baptised increases this difficulty. My own conviction here is that it will not be possible to sustain energy and momentum for our pastoral task unless we address the missionary one. There is something at the heart of church that makes this so – it is in reaching out that we renew what is within. Fr Donovan doesn't mince his words on this point: 'A Christian community that spends all its resources on a building campaign for its own needs has long ago left

Christianity high and dry on the banks' (p. 79). I believe too that the new structures for collaborative ministry will not succeed without a missionary momentum. If there is not a strong outreach, they will atrophy and die.

I think it is fair to say that for most of us involved in church work our energy is pastoral rather than missionary. We find this new missionary context unpleasant and unwelcome, and for the most part we are at a loss for what to do. The notion of putting ourselves on a permanent missionary footing is not something we can contemplate, but that is where I think Fr Donovan is so interesting. His notion of a missionary drive is one that is short, sharp and focused. It is prepared for and then done. I think such an approach could fit in with the rhythm of parish or diocesan life here. A missionary drive could be prepared for, completed and the results integrated into our pastoral ministries. Not at all unlike the old parish 'mission' approach, which came around once a decade and connected once with each new generation.

There is something in Fr Donovan's missionary perspective worth chewing on here. I think there is enormous missionary scope and capacity in our local churches, not sustainable indefinitely, but certainly for periodic initiatives. Our mission does not have to be impossible, if it is impermanent! Of course, one of the very interesting implications of a missionary drive towards the generations that have moved away from church is this: if we accept Fr Donovan's point that their authentic response *is* the church then we cannot be totally prescriptive about the form of parish life that will result from this. There needs to be a sensitive, open conversation; not an old culture imposing its forms on the new.

CHAPTER

10 Status anxiety

There was a documentary on television some time ago exploring how so many people today are worried about their status in the world. It struck me that the programme had something powerfully positive to say about Christian faith in this context. People worry about how they are doing and, more importantly, they worry about how other people think they are doing. This is called 'status anxiety' and it is a feature of modern society. It was not part of traditional societies because there was no real possibility then for upward mobility, and so people felt less responsible for their situation. While they suffered from many things they did not suffer from status anxiety. Religion in that type of society helped people cope with this situation by emphasising the next life over this life. The message was that it did not matter what happened to us in this life – the main thing was to get to heaven and avoid hell.

Today I think most people know that there is something imbalanced, something extreme in that message that does not sit right with them. They believe that this life *is* important. However, they also know that the message from the opposite extreme does not sit right with them either. This is the message of our consumer culture that says that the *only* thing that matters is this life and the only measure of how we are doing in this life is the quantity of material things that we can consume or accumulate. According to this message people's status is measured by the size of their house, their car or their bank balance. I believe there is a hunger in people's hearts for a spiritually balanced life that avoids either of these extremes. Recently I was involved with a series of meditation sessions with confirmation classes during which we asked the children to reflect and share on their hopes for their future. This sense of balance came across powerfully. On the one hand, they wanted to enjoy life and be successful at school and at work. On the other hand, they wanted as part of their lives spiritual values such as friendship, belonging, respect for other people and a relationship with God. The recent O'Donnell study of Irish young adults that I have quoted earlier shows clearly that this desire for a balanced spirituality is still very central – it does not go away with confirmation.

Desiring a balanced spirituality is one thing; living it is another. Status anxiety can push people towards the extremes of materialism even though their hearts really do not want to go there. This is where Christian faith is so relevant. It has some powerful messages that help people achieve a healthy and happy balance in their lives:

- Each of us is a unique, irreplaceable human being, loved by God for who we are. Our worth is not in what material goods or success that we accumulate – we are

priceless because we are made by God and there never has been nor never will be anyone quite like us. We deserve respect and dignity because of this – this is what gives us our primary status as human beings.
- Just as this is true for each one of us, so it is exactly true for everyone else. Every human being deserves our equal respect, no matter what their colour, sex or material status.
- God is with us in our struggle towards a happy, healthy, balanced life. God wants that for us and is there to help us if we ask. Just as God is there for us in this life so too God will be with us in the next life. This is powerfully significant in the face of the consumerist message that the only thing we will ever be is what we achieve here and now. Our Christian faith says this is not true. Yes, we do get on with our lives as best we can, but whatever happens here God still has more in store for us.

I believe these messages are part of the content of evangelisation in today's culture. Our priority as church is to seek to communicate this good news whenever possible – and we are not at all short of opportunities.

Here I must acknowledge that over the years I have worked with many good people in ministry who find this positive perspective a bit hard to take. Their experience has left them doubtful about the reality of a spiritual hunger in contemporary culture. There are two points I would like to make here on this.

Firstly, this invitation to be positive is not an invitation to naiveté. It does not mean being blind to the presence of the gods of war, wealth, power and pleasure in our culture at both systemic and personal levels. What it is saying is that while these gods are powerful, they are not all-powerful. There is within and without the church a sense in people's hearts that we are made for something better. I believe that this sense is deeply resonant of the gospel vision of Jesus and provides an opportunity-in-dialogue for evangelisation. As such it is a trace of the workings of the Spirit today.

Secondly, in order to be able to recognise and respond to this we as church people need to be free of status concerns both at a personal and institutional level. For good and bad reasons to do with the clash between the cultures of modernity and of the church, we find ourselves largely at the margins of popular consciousness today. A great many good, ordinary people find it difficult to read the significance of who we are and of what we do. It is understandable that many of us in ministry are personally hurt by this. We remember a time not too long ago when ours was a central role in the culture, one that was largely understood and appreciated. We find it difficult in the face of indifference not to feel defensive, aggressive or discouraged. This represents a huge challenge to us to develop our personal spiritual foundations, so that we are not dependent on the recognition, approval or gratitude of the popular culture for what we do. This situation may have created in us a sense of grievance or resentment. We may feel something like this: 'We won't have anything to do with these people unless and until our central importance is reinstated!' My gut sense is that being on the margins of twenty-first century culture is a good place to be – it can help us to achieve great clarity and simplicity in regard to what we are about. It certainly does not prevent us from enjoying the good news of the gospel in our own lives and offering that good news to others. Irrespective of how the culture is we can still offer in friendship the gospel as gift because we experience it as good news ourselves, and that is reason enough and thanks enough.

Beyond personal self-esteem and status issues there are also difficulties around institutional status that we need to overcome. For example, our sensitivities regarding the significance of our liturgies and sacraments are often offended by people's sometimes blasé approach to these. We feel that events such as baptisms, first communions and confirmations are sometimes reduced to social occasions with little appreciation of their sacredness among those taking part. Jesus' admonition against 'casting our pearls' comes strongly to mind for us. This can result in taking up the understandable pastoral position of wanting to exclude from the sacraments those who do not seem to display sufficient respect for them.

My sense is that we would need to think carefully about this question. A sense of respect for the sacred in our rituals and sacraments needs to be balanced by a respect for the sacredness of the people coming or, as the case may be, not coming to these. Jesus' admonition that Sabbath was made for man and not man for the Sabbath has something to say to us here as well. While it continues to be the case that our rituals and sacraments are wanted in the culture, they represent opportunities for evangelisation-in-dialogue and we should be slow to cut off these opportunities. There is plenty of evidence for a moral and religious sensibility in the culture that we can build on, even if it is very different from what we were used to or would expect. If we were to stand in judgement over the people regarding their worthiness to receive our sacraments is there not an equal case for the people to stand in judgement over us, on the question of our worthiness to confer?

PART TWO

MINISTRY APPROACHES

Section 1: Evangelisation

CHAPTER

11 Into the deep

'A harbour is a safe place for boats,' says the poster, 'but that's not what boats are built for.' I think there is something in that for our parishes and religious communities today. In his letter 'At the Beginning of the Millennium' Pope John Paul asked us to put out into the deep, to reach out with a new missionary energy to bring the good news of the gospel to the people of our time. His imagery suggests powerfully that we leave the safety of the harbour, the safety of our familiar rounds of pastoral practice.

My sense is that many of us in ministry agree in our heads that this is what is needed; we feel it in our hearts; but we do not seem to be able to act on it. We continue to circle our boats in the safety of the harbour, catching fewer and fewer fish. We continue with the rounds of pastoral practice that we are comfortable with, even though these are connecting with fewer people.

Why do we not move out? I think we need to ask that question of each other and ourselves in a gentle, compassionate way. Any of us that has a religious sense also has a desire to share that sense – it is part of who we are – and at some deep level we hurt when we cannot offer to others what we have experienced as good news for ourselves. So I think there must be good reason why we do not move out.

My own sense is that the reason starts in the heart. The water out there looks choppy. Our boats feel small and fragile. We do not feel skilled or experienced enough to go out. We do not have much of a sense of hope that we will catch anything. In that context it is understandable that we might say, 'Let the fish come into us!' It is also understandable that we make ourselves as busy as possible within the harbour, contenting ourselves with the few fish that come to our nets.

I believe there is a huge spiritual challenge facing us here – to attend to the state of our hearts. We need not do this with anger, frustration or dismissal. We can calmly, quietly notice our fear, our lack of confidence, our lack of hope and begin to look at how we might nourish in one another a sense of hope and courage and confidence. I do not think that this movement into depth comes before any movement out. 'Put out into the deep' (Lk 5:4) suggests that the movement to spiritual depth and the movement towards mission accompany one another. It was through the act of moving out that the fishermen found the heart to become missionaries.

But where to start? Reaching out does not necessarily mean moving immediately into uncharted waters. There are places just a little beyond the mouth of the harbour – relatively safe places – where we can begin. In particular, there are possibilities of liturgies and rituals that connect with key moments in people's lives. I believe these offer parishes very real opportunities, within the scope of our competence, for significant outreach work. There follows a couple of stories that illustrate this point.

★★★

It was a freezing cold Sunday morning. I stood with a group of about sixty people outside a small rural church while a funeral mass was being celebrated inside. We could not get in because the church was already packed. The whole local community and many more besides had gathered to pay final respects to a very popular local octogenarian. A loudspeaker allowed us to hear what was going on inside. While there was some general chitchat among the sixty at the beginning of the mass there was complete silence once the homily begun. The priest told some stories about the deceased that drew smiles. He then raised the question, 'Where is this man now?', and went on to speak in simple, clear terms about what Christians believe about life after death.

It seemed to me that the priest had utilised superbly a teaching moment in a lovely meeting of the gospel and culture. There was great warmth in his words towards the man who had died and towards the family. Blended into this was a Christian theology of the after-life. If he had tried to teach that theology through some formal course very few of the congregation would have come. However, in the context of a funeral they were not only glad to come, but quite happy to stand in the bitter cold in order to hear what he had to say.

★★★

Another story. I was part of a parish group planning a theology programme. We made the arrangements before Christmas for a February start. We planned carefully each detail of the programme and advertised it very well. Only after the programme commenced did it dawn on us that one of the nights coincided with the feast of St Blaise. We had nothing planned for that feast. So at the last moment we found ourselves rushing to organise details in regard to masses and prayer services for the day and we barely managed to get the information into the weekend bulletin. On St Blaise's night some sixty people came to the theology session (it was held in the church). We were very pleased with the attendance, and we had an excellent talk and discussion. Throughout that day in the same church twenty times that number came to the Masses and prayer services to have their throats blessed! What was most striking was the age range. Children, young adults, middle aged and elderly were all there – a much broader mix of people than had attended the theology session.

The final 'blessing of throats' ritual finished in the church just before the theology programme started in the day chapel at the back of the church. There were hundreds of people in the church. So the priest invited them to stay on for the programme. They stayed on all right – to meet and chat with one another, but they hadn't a notion of going back for the theology. I remember looking at them and thinking to myself, 'Instead of trying to bring our people to the theology why in the name of God didn't we think of bringing our theology to the people?

For me these are very ordinary stories that have a profoundly important message for us as church. Being faithful to our call to preach the gospel in today's new culture does not make obsolete all our pastoral traditions. Many of these remain central to our culture and offer us a ready-made opportunity to engage with our task.

CHAPTER

12 A pastoral structure for evangelisation

Our Christian story is a gift that offers us the bigger picture on life. That puts the details of life in perspective and prevents any from dominating and reducing our lives. However, as we know only too well, none of this happens automatically. The challenge of penetrating the depth of the human heart with the good news of the gospel is not easy. There is a great deal of surface agitation and insecurity in all of us. Our insecurities lead us to closing rather than opening our hearts. They lead us to dispositions of hoarding, controlling, distrusting, excluding – the very opposite of the kingdom values. They lead us to missing the bigger picture, the greater possibilities.

That is true not only of those whom we seek to evangelise and catechise, it is also true of us evangelists and catechists. Often our very efforts at offering the gift of the good news are themselves marked by our insecurities. Instead of being servants of the presence of God in the world we seek to be masters of that presence. We seek to own and control the distribution of the grace of God. I

A PASTORAL STRUCTURE FOR EVANGELISATION

think it is certainly true that insecurity has been a mark of how we as church have been present in the modern world. That insecurity has sometimes led us to forms of religious communication that contradict the heart of our religious message. I think it is a sign of the presence of the spirit of God in contemporary culture that many people recognise and resist this religious reductionism. This is perhaps not the only reason why we have trouble communicating our message to day, but it is a significant reason. There is a great challenge for us to open our hearts to the good news of the gospel, and to find ways of effectively communicating our experience of that good news to others.

In this context I think the school catechetical programmes are an encouraging reference point. They represent a sustained, creative effort at communicating the heart of the gospel to children and young people through a medium appropriate to their culture. They reflect very well on our education system and on our society as a whole in that for the most part we recognise the value of and create space for liberating religious education as part of the overall educational and cultural development of each new generation.

But however good the school programmes are, they are not sufficient on their own as a strategy for sparking and sustaining faith in the young. They need to be situated in the supportive context of home and community, and here of course lies a problem. We know anecdotally and from numerous surveys that young parents are increasingly disconnecting from regular contact with their local parishes. We know too that faith is not a matter that many of them broach with their children in their homes. For a great many children the only place where they experience and explore faith is in the classroom with other children. A powerful lesson they may learn from that is that religion is for children; something to be set aside like Santa Clause as soon as they move beyond childhood. Many have already reached that conclusion by the time they arrive at secondary school. In that context it is clear that further, exclusively school-based catechetical programmes have not been and should not be expected to be sufficient in themselves to change this situation.

It is vital that as a church we invest resources in a faith development strategy that can touch the mass of adults and can lead to ongoing opportunities for children, young people and adults together to experience and explore their faith. The school-based programmes offer a model for adult evangelisation and catechesis in the care that they take for culturally appropriate communication and elaboration of the gospel message. They seek to draw out and educate the natural, graced religious sense of the young in a way that connects with their whole lives. They do so in a manner that is appropriate to where the young are at. They recognise and work with the goodness deep in the hearts of the young, their openness to God. That does not mean that the programmes are naïve about failings; that they do not recognise sinfulness. However, their focus is more on the grace of God present in the heart of human nature and their impulse is to celebrate that grace.

I believe the same general approach could be used successfully with adults. And it needs to be done, both as

A PASTORAL STRUCTURE FOR EVANGELISATION

an end in itself and as a necessary accompaniment to the school-based programmes. We need to develop a comprehensive adult programme that recognises and seeks to build on the grace deep in the heart of contemporary culture. A programme not naïve to the sinfulness of our culture but focused first on offering our good news, on revealing more clearly the beautiful presence of God already amongst us.

Few might disagree with that but many will raise the question of the structure within which it can be done. The school system provides a ready-made framework for the catechetical programmes that allows us to connect with the mass of each generation. But only a tiny percentage of adults attend adult religious education courses. This is only a problem if we stay narrowly focused on formal education models. What we need to do is attend to the wider and utterly obvious opportunities for mass evangelisation and catechetical work with adults available to us at key ritual moments that continue to be widely popular. At the heart of faith is the *experience* of God, not simply information about God. Ritual offers a richer environment for fostering and exploring that experience than does a classroom. I do not for a moment deny the place and value of academic discipline, but for most adults their theology will be formed in the context of ritual or not at all.

There is a cycle of popular religious rituals that could offer a very concrete framework for a planned, focused faith-development drive among adults and, especially, among young parents; a drive that would have a strong evangelisation stamp; a drive that could be planned for, delivered over a few years and then evaluated. The ritual moments that make up the elements of this framework range from Christmas, Lent, Easter and November rituals to weddings, baptisms and funerals, to first communions and confirmations, to novenas, anniversary masses, blessing of throats, end of school year masses and so on.

Just as we carefully plan the curriculum and methodology of the school catechetical programmes to fit into the school environment and connect with the culture of the children, so too we could plan an adult programme to fit into the pattern of these rituals and connect with the culture of the adults. We could plan how homily, music, prayer, silence and the distinctive features of each ritual could all contribute within this programme. We have many of the elements already tried and tested. What is missing is some joined-up thinking that could pull them together into a comprehensive adult faith-development programme to complement and support the school programmes.

Have we the financial and human resources to deliver such a programme? Money-wise, I suspect we could develop and deliver a national programme of adult evangelisation and catechesis over a number of years for less than what it would cost to renovate one cathedral and for a lot less than the financial pay-out arising from the abuse scandals. Personnel-wise, we have a great many people in the country – priests, religious and lay people – who have energy and capacity around liturgy. I believe they would have great enthusiasm for a programme that utilised popular liturgical moments for evangelisation and catechesis, especially one directed at those who have

A PASTORAL STRUCTURE FOR EVANGELISATION

disconnected from church. Obviously they would need training and support, but they are already on home territory here, playing to their strengths.

We have been talking for years about adult faith development; about the need to foster home and parish as partners with our schools in the task of handing on our Christian story. If we only bit the bullet on this we could be profoundly surprised and delighted by what we achieve. Instead of mourning the decline of faith and church we could be celebrating the Spirit of God alive and well in our twenty-first century church and culture!

CHAPTER

13 Horses for courses

Finding effective approaches to adult faith formation has been a strong concern in many parishes over the years and has resulted in quite a range of pastoral initiatives. Reflecting on my own work experience in that area and on the experience of many parish renewal groups and parish leadership groups, it seems to me that there are some patterns coming through in those experiences that cast some light on what works and does not work, and offer some general directions for further work.

The faith formation initiatives broadly seem to fall into two mutually complementary categories. One category is small-group based and includes a range of prayer groups, scripture reflection groups, religious education programmes etc. These tend to run on a regular basis with a small number of people taking part. The other category is large-group based, is mainly liturgical in form or connected in some way with the sacraments, and tends to run occasionally or seasonally. Here I'm thinking of events such as novenas, sacramental meetings, masses for the dead and for other special occasions.

The first category broadly speaking is continuous but not popular; the second category is popular but not continuous. I think this distinction offers a useful way of thinking about and planning for adult faith formation initiatives in our parishes. It might also help us to avoid holding unrealistic and ultimately discouraging expectations in regard to these initiatives. Frequently our efforts at the small group, continuous model are criticised because they don't attract large groups; and our efforts at the popular approaches are criticised because they are not continuous – 'Where's the follow-up?'.

My sense is that, realistically, any strategy for adult faith formation needs to include both categories but both need to be judged in their own terms.

There are certain church events that are popular but not continuous (i.e. baptisms, weddings, funerals, confirmations, first communions, Christmas liturgies, Ash Wednesday, Feast of St Blaise etc.). The majority of people participate in these. Other church events are continuous but not popular (prayer groups, ministry group activities, adult religious-education programmes etc.) Generally, less than 10 per cent of people attend these. It is these less popular events that the 'C's attend. Their lives are inserted into a rhythm of religion. It is the more popular ones that the 'A's and 'B's are most drawn to – religion is inserted into the rhythm of their lives at key moments. A hugely liberating learning for me from this was that I should look to the popular type of event as the principal strategy in doing evangelisation work with 'A' groups.

My experience is that the 'market' for small-group initiatives is a limited one, somewhere between 5 and 10 per cent of the adult population. I think it is very important that we seek to create an environment in our parishes where a variety of small-group approaches can be present for this section of the population, but without carrying the expectation that everybody will take part. It is also my experience that the small-group initiatives take a large amount of energy and time to run and the ones that survive are those that have a small core group of people who are passionate about what they are doing. I think that this has practical implications for parish leadership groups. We can introduce a range of small-group opportunities. Some will take root in the parish in the sense that a number of people will emerge who are committed to sustaining them. When that happens it is great and it is important to allow those who have the energy to run with the initiative. Other initiatives will not take root in this way. Here the parish leadership group needs to have the courage, sooner or later, to let go.

I hope I am not sounding defeatist here when I suggest that 90 to 95 per cent of the adult population will successfully resist any attempts to engage them in small-group, continuous models of faith formation. It is my experience that there is a very widespread openness to occasional or seasonal pastoral initiatives and these provide our best bet in terms of a strategy for popular faith formation. Here the challenge for parish leadership groups is to be alert for locally appropriate opportunities – whether to do with celebrating the harvest, remembering the dead, blessing small children, celebrating a local saint, celebrating Christmas and so on. I think the huge attraction for these (both for those who participate and those who organise) is that they are not continuous, but can be planned for and carried out as once-per-year events. They can be part of the annual parish calendar.

For me the picture of the immediate future of adult faith formation is a kind of 'mesh' of initiatives, some small-group and continuous, others popular and occasional. This state of affairs can be sustained by leadership groups in the medium term at least if the small-group initiatives can run on their own steam and if the popular initiatives can be reasonably spread out over the year.

CHAPTER

14 Evangelisation as dialogue

Bilingual ministries

At a Limerick diocesan assembly of priests and laity, Michael Paul Gallagher SJ offered his vision for evangelisation in contemporary Irish society. His starting point was the belief that our capacity as church to communicate our good news to the wider culture has been significantly lessened by recent cultural change. Our language and symbols no longer communicate effectively: 'A whole language of faith is dying, but then it is the adventure of church history to create new languages for our good news for new cultures.' We need to become what he terms 'pastorally bilingual', able to appreciate the older language of devotion and church but able to speak also to and from the newer wavelength of experience, story and spirituality. This would allow us to include and engage the experience of the culture with the good news of the gospel. However, in order to so reach out we may have to first reach in, to see to what extent the traumas of the last decade have left those of us in ministry 'suffering from unrecognised cultural desolation'. Only in getting in touch with and supporting one another in our hurt hopes will we find the energy to reach out in fresh ways to the new situation.

Michael Paul offers the practice of Jesus with his disciples on the road to Emmaus (Lk 24:13-35) as a six-step model for this reaching out:

1 Jesus walked by their side – his starting point was simply being with them
2 Jesus asked them, 'What matters are you discussing?' He asked for and listened to *their* interpretation of *their* experience
3 Having listened, Jesus then responded, offering his interpretation of their experience, his good news
4 Then Jesus 'made as if to go on' – he left them with the freedom to invite him in or not
5 Jesus broke bread with them in response to their invitation
6 They then 'returned to Jerusalem' – reconnecting with their church.

It seems to me that this approach offers a very liberating and challenging perspective on evangelisation in Ireland today, one very amenable to concrete pastoral application. In the first place it says that reconnecting with the church is an outcome of rather than a pre-condition for evangelisation, an outcome chosen or not by people in freedom. I believe it means putting our energy into finding and utilising as best we can opportunities for evangelisation, and feeling free then to leave the people with the choice of how they want to respond. Secondly, it says that *evangelisation is not a monologue.* It is not simply a matter of us, using our language and our symbols, getting the people to 'shut up and listen'. Instead evangelisation is a conversation, an invitation for people to bring their story and their interpretation of it into a sacred space, and engaging with that story, bringing our sense of the good news of the gospel to it.

I have mentioned that key transition moments in people's lives currently provide and will continue to provide for the foreseeable future our best opportunities for evangelisation – they are the moments when the mass of the people are very open to engaging with church. What approach do we bring to these opportunities? Take, for example, funerals. Here more than any place else there is an opportunity for a 'bilingual' encounter between the depth of the culture and the depth of the gospel. Funeral times represent a sacred space within which the profound experience of the loss of a loved one can be expressed and interpreted by the people, and in that context the good news of the gospel offered. This does not mean replacing the gospel stories with stories from the culture, it simply means including the cultural stories and explicitly bringing the gospel to bear on them.

It seems to me that many pastorally sensitive people in ministry are caught between a desire for an appropriate bilingual approach on the occasion of the funeral and the official church position, which is quite strictly 'monolingual'. This latter approach assumes that our words and symbols are adequate to communicate a religious interpretation of the occasion and so seeks to minimise or exclude the voice, the symbols, the music of the people – regarding these as intrusions into and distractions from the task. I believe that this sense of liturgical correctness represents a serious pastoral mistake. It means we miss the opportunity to connect with the depth experience of the people, to hear and honour their sacred story and to evangelise that story with the story of the gospel. In thus seeking to silence the people we run the serious risk of alienating their depth experiences from the gospel, leaving our liturgies and our words up in the air rather than rooted in and growing from their experience.

Just as with funerals, so too with weddings, baptisms, first communions and confirmations we experience the tensions between the simpler 'mono-lingual' pastoral approach and the 'bilingual' approach. It seems to me that there is already a wide variety of bilingual approaches in practice on the ground and that the experience of these needs to be brought into conversation with our theology of sacraments and liturgy.

A listening church

In these times of great change for the church in Ireland the notion of a popular religious culture here might seem at first glance a contradiction in terms. Regular attendance at weekly mass now a minority practice, the collapse of vocations, the shift in public practice from church teaching on matters to do with family and sexuality – all these and more would suggest that religion is anything but popular. Yet at the same time the churches are packed at Christmas; pre-Christmas reconciliation liturgies in many parishes draw great crowds; and sacramental occasions continue to have a very high profile in the life cycle of families and communities. Is there a contradiction here? I do not think so.

What has happened is that up to recent decades there was a substantial alignment between the popular and the institutional in regard to religious practice. Now the culture has shifted and the close alignment is gone. There is now much in what is institutionally prescribed that is no longer culturally popular. In place of an alignment we can speak of an overlap. Substantial elements of institutional practice continue to be popular. Many of us church people are decidedly unimpressed by this overlap. We dismiss it with the term 'à la carte'. We might even prefer if those who occupy the overlap space would move off it all together and leave the church to those who are prepared to stay fully aligned. This reaction is understandable – when so many people dismiss what we regard as vital to church life it is natural that we might in turn dismiss what they regard as vital.

However, I think it is important to pay close, respectful attention to the popular religious culture. One of the root meanings of worship is to gather around that which is held as having worth. This meaning offers a very interesting perspective on religious practice. Popular gatherings in our churches point to widely and deeply held feelings of what is held worthy by the people. They indicate where our practices are still overlapping with 'the joy and hope, the grief and anguish of the people of our time'. Likewise the decline in certain practices indicates a disconnection of those practices from what is felt as worthwhile in people's lives.

There is a range of possibilities facing the church in Ireland in the coming decades. On one end of the range, we could become a well-defined, elitist remnant in the culture, out of touch with and insignificant in the lives of the great mass of people. On the other end, we could be a popular church, connected into the lives of the majority of people, struggling to bring the gospel to bear on those lives with all the messiness and incompleteness that this would entail. I hope for the latter. The present popular religious culture suggests that that is possible.

I believe that this religious culture can be deepened and widened; that there are many more areas in people's lives and a much broader sense of worth that our worship gatherings could overlap with. The key starting point is to attend to what people today hold to be of worth and to struggle with the question of how that sense of worth can be brought into a deeper encounter with the good news of the gospel. But here we need to recognise that this entails a *two-way* teaching process.

One of these ways is one we understand readily enough – that we teach the people. We teach them the good news of the gospel, the meaning of the sacraments, the symbols and so on. The other way may not be so obvious to us – that we allow the people to teach us. Teach us what? About their lives. About what they hold to be of worth in their lives, about their hurts and hopes, their joys and sorrows. And why would we do that? So that we can be in a better position to struggle with the question of how those lives can be brought into a deeper encounter with the good news of the gospel. So that we can explore what language, what symbols can better communicate our good news.

This perspective on evangelisation may not be a comforting one for us because it suggests that we may need to learn a new language to effectively communicate our good news today; because it suggests that in sticking faithfully (and exclusively) to the religious language and symbols that have been passed down to us we may end up being unfaithful to our core task of evangelisation.

One of the pastoral tools that I have found most useful in getting in touch with what is going on in people's lives, and one that is easy to work with, is the listening survey. Basically it involves a systematic listening to people and noticing what it is that engages their attention. What is it they speak about with strong feelings – of anger, sadness, joy and hope? What activities do they engage in with most energy? Normally a listening survey is conducted by a small number of people in the community and of the community. They meet on an agreed number of occasions. The agenda is simple: they share what it is they noticed people speak about or engage with during the week with strong feelings. They do not go around with a questionnaire; they are not spying on other people's conversations; they are simply going about their day-to-day business, taking part in the conversations and activities that they normally do. The only difference is that they are alert to the strong feelings they encounter and they bring what they have heard back to their meeting. At this meeting they are not talking about named individuals – they are talking about issues that they noticed the people caring about. Sometimes a listening survey is focused on a particular group – young people, Travellers, women, men, young parents or the elderly, for example. In such cases the group doing the listening is drawn mainly from that group.

Over a number of meetings a clear picture builds up of the reality of people's lives in the community. Strong themes emerge. Some of these themes will offer concrete contact points for evangelisation. A sensitive pastoral group in a parish can then explore how best these contact points could be developed. A starting point would be to look within the popular religious culture for opportunities. For instance, a parish interested in evangelisation work with young parents could start with the parish baptism programme. In the light of a listening survey among young parents the group might explore the question of how that programme can be developed to create a deeper connection between the concerns of the parents and the good news of the gospel. It seems to me that there are a great number of ministries going on in the parishes that could benefit in this way from a listening survey.

CHAPTER 15

Sunday mass

I feel it is clear that in very many parishes we can and do avail of special or seasonal moments to provide liturgy experiences that connect well with large numbers of people. Our difficulty is doing this week-in and week-out.

We were used to a situation where it did not matter what was done or not done at Sunday mass – people still came. Nor did it matter what else was happening in their lives: mass attendance had such a priority that everything else was organised around it. While this situation still holds true today for most of the older section of the population, there has been a massive shift among the majority of the younger half. For them, church-related activities occupy a position somewhere at the margins of their consciousness. This is not a rigidly fixed position. Church can and does move occasionally from the margins towards the centre depending on what is happening in their lives. But the point is that participation in church activities increasingly depends more on the circumstances of their lives than on what is going on in the church.

What we have to respond to then is not simply a change from regular practice to non-practice, but to circumstantial practice. For some, circumstantial practice means that they will continue to go to mass normally, unless there is something else on that particular weekend. For example, our mass attendance on the weekend of a World Cup final fell by over 15 per cent! (I think this pattern may account at least for some of the disparity between the national statistics on mass attendance and the actual numbers present in any parish on a given weekend.) For others, circumstantial practice means that they will not normally attend liturgy unless it is connecting with something else that is going on in their lives.

Most of us in ministry are, of course, not very happy with the fact that what we do is increasingly marginal. We are not comfortable with the notion of having to compete for people's attention with many other events and influences that often seem to be more central for them. We believe that the weekend mass *should* be a priority and that we should not have to go to any extra lengths to get people to come. Yet we see clearly that this is no longer the case and we are left with the question, 'What do we do?'

My own sense is that the circumstantial pattern of attendance offers us a clue as to how to respond. People are sensitive to and responsive to liturgy that connects with their lives. They feel free not to attend liturgy that they experience as unconnected to them. Some time ago I was involved in a parish survey about people's experience of the weekend liturgy. The survey was conducted among both regular and irregular attenders. The feedback was clear, challenging and troubling.

For those who have stopped going to mass the reason offered was that mass was simply not relevant to them; it did not touch their lives or their sense of the spiritual. While for some, spirituality was a vague, relatively unimportant matter, for others it was an important part of their lives. For us then the question was not only, 'What's wrong with them that they have stopped engaging with our weekend liturgies?' but also 'What's wrong with our weekend liturgies that they no longer engage these people?'

From among the regular attenders, two quite different messages came out. Among the over-45s who regularly attend mass the basic position was *leave well enough alone!* They are content with mass as they find it. The message from young people still attending regularly was exactly the opposite: they do not enjoy going, they do not look forward to going, they do not find the mass relevant, they cannot offer a compelling reason why they go. Their continued regular attendance is seriously in doubt. This feedback posed dilemmas: What do the people mean when they say mass is irrelevant? How can we respond without alienating those who say we should leave things as they are?

A second piece of research that I referred to earlier was helpful with these questions. A study of the prayers placed in petition boxes in a shopping centre as part of the lead up to a Novena to St Therese provided us with some insights into people's spirituality and the issues in their lives that they regard as relevant to prayer. The overwhelming majority of the prayers was focused on daily life concerns (immediate family or personal issues such as health, relationships, life crises etc.). The primary expression of their spirituality was in their relationships – a very strong sense of loving and caring came across. Further, it was clear that the people welcomed opportunities to bring the concerns of their lives and relationships to prayer, through the saints, to God. Thinking or praying about faith came across as a minority concern. For the majority, religion was something they did rather than reflected on. (It was not surprising then that while over 2,000 people attended each session of the Novena, only 50 people came to a subsequent adult religious education meeting about saints!) The second thing that was powerfully striking was the language of the prayers – simple, direct, immediate and concrete – and such a contrast to the language of our liturgies!

I think this throws some light on the question of what people mean when they say that mass is irrelevant. Liturgy that ignores human relationships is going to have great difficulty connecting with the people. For most people, religion is experienced as relevant to the extent that it is in relationship to their life concerns. They are most open to experiences of prayer and ritual when these are connected with their concerns and expressed in their language. There is very limited interest in religious information *per se*. There is a yawning gap between the language and theology of our liturgies, and the language and theology of our people. Unless and until we bridge that gap the ongoing and I think rapid decline in weekly mass attendance will continue.

One of the ways that parishes have sought to explore this possible avenue is through developing particular liturgy styles that seek to resonate more with particular groups. This variety in mass style is more possible of course in urban situations where there are a number of masses in the parish. So we have children's masses, youth masses, gospel masses, candlelight masses, Irish masses, Latin masses and so on.

I believe that these efforts are important and that we should monitor their impact over a period. In one parish I worked in we drew on this approach to develop a variety of mass styles for the regular Sundays. This includes a candlelight mass at 8.30 p.m., a children's mass at 10.00 a.m. and a 'gospel' mass on the second and fourth Sundays of the month at 1.00 p.m.

Another approach has been the development of themed weekend liturgies. The *Do This In Memory* programme involves a series of weekend liturgies connected with preparation for first communion. It has proven very successful as a way of connecting parents into the sacramental preparation of their children. I believe that one of the reasons for this success is its utilisation of a familiar setting for the parents – the weekend liturgy. While the majority of young parents are not regular mass goers they have shown themselves far more likely to participate in religious formation initiatives set in the context of parish liturgy rather than, say, in adult education.

I have seen this pattern repeat itself at many other moments. Young adults will come in great numbers to a gospel choir mass, parents will come to a blessing of children mass, all age groups will come to a mass that includes the sacrament of reconciliation. However, one of the difficulties that comes with this is that the standard form of the liturgy is itself the product of a particular culture and this often clashes with the culture of the congregation. Very often the language and imagery of the liturgy do not communicate with those present and so the central core of the liturgy gets lost in a welter of obscure detail.

For example, I have often seen a church packed with young parents and their children – all present for the annual parish blessing of small children. They seem to relate to the blessing and the consecration, sometimes the homily; the rest they endure. I wonder in these circumstances whether a radical simplification of the liturgy would not make sense. Earlier I touched on the book *Christianity Rediscovered*. I was powerfully struck by what Fr Donovan had to say on this point.

> So the first masses in the new Masai communities were simplicity itself. I would take bread and wine, without any preceding or following ritual and say to the people – 'This is the way it was passed on to me, and I pass it on to you that on the night before he died, Jesus took bread and wine into his hands, blessed them and said, "This is my body. This is the cup of my blood of the new Covenant, poured out for the forgiveness of sins. Do this in my memory".' That served as Offertory, Preface and Canon. The people took it from there. (p. 91)

I am not a liturgist but it seems to me only common sense that the form of the liturgy should be significant for the people. There are many occasions when the standard form is significant. Daily mass and early Sunday morning masses are often at the positive end of the spectrum in this regard. There the form of the liturgy and the faith of the people seem to connect simply and profoundly. Weddings and funerals are often at the other end of the spectrum. Does it make sense to have a single form of liturgy for all?

What I found hugely attractive about Fr Donovan was his courage and clarity in confronting this question in his missionary context. His first priority was the communication and celebration of the good news to the people – everything else, including the form of liturgy, was a function of this. I think that Fr Donovan's spirit is hugely needed in Ireland today.

I am not suggesting here that there should be a free for all or 'anything goes' approach to liturgy; only that there should be a careful paying of attention to and exploration of what does and does not communicate. If I may say this without causing offence, I believe that such an exploration should not be controlled by liturgists, either in Rome or in Ireland; they certainly should be part of the exploration, but in (humble!) conversation with missionaries and pastors, lay and clerical alike. Liturgy is the servant, and potentially a gifted servant, of mission; not its master.

CHAPTER

16   Our music of the gospel

Here I want to look at the possibilities of faith development work with young parents. I have been parenting for twenty years. This has brought me into regular contact with other parents and has left me with a very strong regard for the quality of commitment among them to rear their children as best they can. Over the last decade I have had the opportunity to work directly with young parents in the area of faith development – firstly with Veritas in exploring the question of where they are at and how parishes might respond and, more recently, as a member of the parish team attempting to put into practice some of the findings from this exploration. This overall experience has left me feeling quite upbeat and hopeful in regard to what can be done in this field.

But I think evangelisation work with young parents requires a certain imagination – to appreciate their qualities, to see the connections between those qualities and the good news of the gospel. I would like to start first with an example of that imagination from the music world:

> More than thirty years ago I had a dream…to spread the gospel about Irish music and what it really was. Because a lot of people thought it all started and ended with 'When Irish Eyes are Smiling' and 'Does your Mother come from Ireland?' – all those tearjerkers. But there's more to it than that…it's great, great music…' (Glatt, 1991, p. 264)

So spoke Paddy Moloney looking back on his career with The Chieftains. What strikes me most here is Maloney's confidence in the capacity of traditional Irish music to touch right into the heart of contemporary culture. He saw Irish music not as over and against the wider musical culture, but as a gift enabling that culture to better appreciate its own grace and depth. So when Marijohn Wilkin, author of the country music song 'The Long Black Veil', heard her song interpreted by The Chieftains she said, 'I just sat there and cried because every ounce of my heritage came through in that melody. Listening to The Chieftain's album I thought, "And they wonder where country music comes from"…' (Glatt, p. 293).

Here we have a beautiful metaphor for inculturating the gospel; for bringing the music of our own religious tradition into the mainstream of contemporary culture; for making connections between the deepest inspirations of the culture and the vision of the gospel. I think the church could take a few leaves out of Paddy Moloney's book here. Not just his zeal for evangelisation or his confidence in the good news he brings, but also his friendliness towards the wider culture, his sense of harmonising with all that is best in that culture without at all compromising on the integrity and quality of his own tradition.

This, of course, raises the question of a gospel critique of culture. I am not suggesting that this is not an essential function of the church; what I am drawing attention to here is the *spirit* of Paddy Maloney's approach; his starting point is his *good* news. He looks first for the possibilities of making connections, of creating moments of shared celebration. He is not at all elitist, defensive or aggressive in his approach to the wider culture. I think that same spirit would serve us well, especially in our work of evangelising young parents.

Finding a toe-hold

For some years I was a member of a parish team in Tullamore that attempted in this spirit to reach out to young parents. Our strategy was to create a basic structure of contact built around key moments in the lives of the children. We planned to use that contact for evangelisation purposes and to provide opportunities for the parents to follow up on that if they wished. Concretely this structure of contact consists mainly of the following:

- A series of outreach nights centred on baptism, Junior Infants, first communion and confirmation
- A weekly family mass supplemented with special family masses at Christmas, Easter and at end of the school year
- A 'blessing of small children' mass during the annual novena.

- *Baptism*
  The baptism programme has been in place for a number of years. Originally it consisted of a talk using a series of slides. The content was mainly catechetical, outlining the meaning of the sacrament and the various elements of the ceremony. That was changed to a video with a strong evangelisation content, focusing more on the good news of the gospel for the children and parents and highlighting how this good news connects with the parents' hopes for their children. This night is run monthly throughout the year by a trained baptism team and it is normal for most parents to attend.

- *Junior Infants*
  The night for parents of junior infants began life as an adult education meeting. The parents were invited to the school for a talk and video presentation on the *Alive-O* religion programme. In the first pilot we were powerfully struck by how much the parents were attracted to and delighted by the *Alive-O* approach to teaching religion. The underlying message in the school programme – 'The glory of God is the human person fully alive' – corresponded very well with their own hopes for their children. After the initial pilot we decided to supplement the night with video footage of their own children engaging with the religion programme in the classroom. The talk given had a strong evangelisation content, as in the baptism programme, but it also highlighted three positive things the parents could do to support the faith in their

children: continuing to love them; taking an interest in their religious involvements both in school and in parish; and seeking to develop their own adult spirituality.

In the first year some 120 parents took part in the nights. The breakdown here was roughly one parent per child for the rural and middle-class areas, and one parent for every three children in the working class areas. The evaluations were very positive. However, we felt we would need to rework the format to create a broader appeal.

In year two we recast the nights from parent education to family celebration events marking the completion of the children's first term in school. The junior infants were invited to come along with parents and other family members. We used the video of the children as the main selling point. We did the talk in a shorter format and built in a para-liturgy and a party (see next chapter). The number of parents that took part rose to over 200 and the evaluations were more enthusiastic.

In year three we changed the venue from the schools to the day chapel in the parish church. The numbers of parents attending went up again, this time to 300, with virtually every child having at least one parent there. What was interesting here was that the highest ratio of adults to children came from the working class areas. Our learning was that the more the initiative shifted from formal education to ritual and celebration, the broader was the appeal. The 'talk' input on the night fitted in very well with the video and para-liturgy elements, and was amplified rather than restricted by them.

- *First communion*
  By year three the junior infant children from the first year of the initiative were preparing for their first communion. So we returned to their classrooms, took some footage of them doing their communion preparation and added that to their footage from Junior Infants. We held these nights early on in the school year, again in the day chapel. The format of the nights was again video, talk, para-liturgy and party. The focus of the talk was again evangelisation, affirmation of parents and challenge to parents to respond, and especially to engage with their children's religion programme in the run up to first communion. As with the junior infant nights, we were delighted with the spirit of the gatherings and the positive approach of the parents. Roughly 300 parents came to these nights.

- *Confirmation*
  For a number of years our approach had been to invite the parents to a talk in a local hotel with a guest speaker. This would normally be attended by around 150 parents. We also held commitment ceremonies on a school-by-school basis. In recent years we attempted a new format, taking each of the schools on a separate night and again locating the sessions in the day chapel rather than the schools. Our basic goal was to create a three-way conversation between parents, students and parish team on the relevance of confirmation in the

lives of the students. (See Chapter 18 for details on the shape of the night.)

A number of points struck me from this. Firstly, the number of parents attending went up to about 300, double the number attending the confirmation talk. What featured strongly in their evaluation of the night was how much they enjoyed the opportunity for conversation with their children during the session. Secondly, a central feature of the preparation for the night was a meditation programme with the students. What this brought home to me forcefully was the truth of Vincent McNamara's assertion that we all have soul. Once the students entered into a meditative space they were able to access their own deep hopes and desires for their lives. These were hugely positive and it was not at all difficult to connect these with the gospel vision for their lives. Thirdly, it has been possible to utilise this moment as a bridge into second level. A series of follow-up meditation programmes are currently running with the junior cycle classes.

- *Weekly and special family masses*
  Normally the family masses feature music and artwork from *Alive-O* in the main chapel, with a special liturgy of the word for small children in the day chapel. We had been watching attendances here with interest to see if we could register any impact from the parent nights. While total attendance at these nights came to about two thousand this year (including parents, children and other family members), attendance at the family mass ranged from 600 to 700. Growth here has been very

slow and is mainly seen in increased numbers involved in the children's choir and in children's involvement in other parts of the liturgy. When the children are involved, the parents generally come as well.

For the special liturgies, however, where we put in an extra effort in terms of promotion and creative involvement, the number attending has grown substantially. Generally at these masses all the children in the church are invited up to the altar to sing one of their songs, to bring up a gift or to receive a gift. A letter of invitation goes home through the primary schools.

What this is suggesting broadly is that the parents in the 'A' category did not shift en masse into the 'B' category. However, they did become more regular 'A's with an increased pattern of contact with the local church. They did respond to occasional opportunities to explore and express their faith with their children.

- *Conclusions*

The above describes a work still in progress. The hoped-for outcomes are that the parents will see the relevance of faith to their lives and the lives of their children, and in response will look to deepen their own faith, engage with the faith of their children and worship with the parish. We can control the quality of inputs in regard to how we present the faith, but of course we cannot determine the outcomes. That has always been the case with the evangelisation work of the church. It seems to me now that this much at least is clear in regard to parish work with young parents: we have very good news to offer them and we have the opportunities to invite them to 'come and see'. They are prepared to take up these invitations. Where it goes from there we will have to see. Like Paddy Moloney, I feel optimistic that once they hear our music of the gospel they will like it. Just as he was fired by the possibility of traditional Irish music taking up its place in the mainstream of twenty-first century culture so too we can be fired by the hope of faith being part and parcel of the good, healthy lives of ordinary twenty-first century parents and their children.

CHAPTER

17 An evangelisation moment with parents

I mentioned earlier my belief that the *Alive-O* Primary School religion programme is particularly effective in communicating a foundational sense of the Good News, not just for the children, but also for their parents. I have seen over and again how powerfully parents are touched by video footage of what the children are doing in their religion programme and also by their willingness to turn up in very large numbers when the opportunity is afforded. So when they do turn up what do we say to them? How do we attempt evangelisation? The following is a summary of a talk given to parents of junior infants who came to a celebration night for the pupils on completion of their first term. The night, as described in the last chapter, consisted of some video footage of the children in the classroom, followed by the talk, a short prayer service and a party.

AN EVANGELISATION MOMENT WITH PARENTS

The religion programme is on your side!
This night celebrates a very significant moment in the lives of the children: they have completed their first ever term in school. They are beginning to grow up – to move on in life. As parents you have such deeply felt hopes for the future of these children – that they will grow up as happy, whole, confident human beings, with a sense of life, a sense of fun, a sense of optimism about their place in the world, able to connect well with people, to have good friends and to be a good friend.

The religion programme that the children will be doing over the next eight years is called *Alive-O*. This title is based on the very old religious insight that what God wants for us as human beings is that we become fully alive. And this is the point I want to put to you tonight – when you touch on your deepest hopes for your child the religion programme is on your side. It has the same hopes, the same desires. It can be a real support to you in your task of parenting your child.

Three messages that help your children
There are three powerfully positive messages for the children underpinning the religion programme. The first could be summarised as simply as this – God believes in you! Over and over again the children are learning through games, music and activities this message – God is delighted with

you! God loves you for who you are! God has given each of you special gifts! The second message can be summarised thus – we are happiest when we care for one another. Through all sorts of interactivity the children learn that it is great to have friends and to be a friend. They are being put in touch in an age-appropriate way with the profound insight that as we are made in the image of God, and as God is love, then loving is at the very core of our nature. The third message is that God is our friend who wants us to stay in touch. Here the children are taught skills in how to be in contact with God through moments of quiet, of prayer, of ritual.

It seems to me then that the religion programme at its best offers a very rich vision of who we are as human beings – a vision communicated in a way that the children can and do grasp. Relationships with self, others and God are held together in a balanced way that can offer the children a very positive, healthy foundation for their personal development.

Supporting the religion programme

So, if you accept my point that the religion programme supports at a very deep level your own task of parenting then this raises the question – how can you support the work of the programme? I want to offer three ways:

1 **Your love** – the most powerful spiritual gift you give to your children is your love for them.

AN EVANGELISATION MOMENT WITH PARENTS

Talking about a God who believes in them won't make a lot of sense unless they have already experienced that belief in significant adults in their lives. And overwhelmingly you do a great job here – your children know that you love them and the importance of this in their lives cannot be overstated.

2 **Your interest** – the second way you can support their religious sense is by taking an interest in it. The children are deeply engaged by and comfortable with their religion programme – for them religion is a natural, easy and delightful part of their world. Whatever the children are interested in it is hugely important to them that their parents acknowledge and engage with it. This is true whether it is a toy, a television programme or religion. I think this does present a difficulty for many parents, because while the children are relaxed and easy about religion for the most part, we adults are not! While most of us have held on to a sense of the spiritual our experiences in life have left us at least somewhat disconnected from church and organised religion. However, coming here tonight is a powerful sign of your willingness to support your child's religious sense despite this. I ask you to hold on to this attitude. Be willing to keep giving some of your time and attention to your child's religious development. There will be a lovely children's liturgy here as part of our Christmas (Easter) celebrations. Please do not

deny the children an opportunity to experience this!

3. **Your own growth** – thirdly, if you want your children to grow up as whole, happy and healthy human beings you can help them greatly by trying to become that yourselves. Whatever you do to enhance your own personal development is good for the children. Let them grow up in homes where they experience the adults around them as confident, caring persons. Just as you include the religious dimension in your care for your child so too you can include it in your care for yourself. Research shows clearly that today's young parents have a strong sense of the spiritual, but it is often kept very private and very silent. Our religious sense is a precious part of us and whatever we can do to enhance it is good for us. As we move closer to Christmas (Easter) I ask you to think about that. See if somewhere deep inside you there is a desire to express your religious sense more. The ceremonies coming up in the parish might be a very good place for you to start, with your children.

CHAPTER

18 Evangelising pre-teens

What is it you do not like about the school religion programme? I raised this question in a sixth class group. 'The questions and answers,' was the quick reply. 'Do you not want to learn about your religion?' I asked. One boy stood up at the back of the room and said, 'We don't mind the questions. What we don't like is having to learn off by heart other people's answers!'

This twelve year old is articulating a critique of the church's approach to teaching the good news – one representative of a strong stream in contemporary culture. He is expressing a wish to enter into a conversation about the deep questions of life rather than being the object of a monologue. He believes he has something to contribute to that conversation.

Church people I think generally respond in two different ways to this. Some hold in suspicion the claims of the culture to be really interested in depth questions. They fear that materialism and individualism have so de-spiritualised the culture that any attempt to accommodate it will only result in a dilution of the message that we have been entrusted with by God. So the sense here is this: 'We have to preach the gospel as we have been given it; if people cannot hear it or accept it, so be it. After all, Jesus experienced that same rejection.' Other church people take a more positive view of the culture and believe that the issue is less people's unwillingness to hear the good news and more our inability to communicate that good news properly. So the sense here is this: 'Let's explore new approaches to evangelisation – let's experiment to see what connects with the people.'

My sense is that both responses have something to offer and that the truth rests somewhere in between them. Both arise out of a concern for keeping the integrity of the gospel – one fearing the consequences of too deep an immersion into the culture, the other fearing the consequences of not moving in deeply enough. Seen this way they can be mutually corrective if mutually respectful; if one side does not seek to appropriate exclusive domicile on the high spiritual ground at the expense of the other.

I make this point as a preliminary to offering an example of an attempt at conversational evangelisation with twelve year olds. The setting was a series of commitment ceremonies for the confirmation classes in a parish. The classes had already been approached some time earlier by the school chaplains with this request: 'Will you participate in a meditation programme in preparation for your confirmation – one that will allow you to create posters about the values that are really important to you? Will you also come to a confirmation meeting with your parents so that we can talk about these values?' The sixth classes responded very well; both boys and girls took easily

to the meditations and the parent nights. Each school had their own night and the parents were invited. The format of the nights was as follows:
1. Presentation of student posters
2. Response by parish on the relevance of confirmation to the values in these posters
3. Quiet time for students to fill in confirmation commitment cards
4. Sharing these cards with their parents
5. Prayer service
6. Refreshments.

While the content of the posters varied, the underlying values remained fairly constant: be yourself, be true to your friends, be true to God. The responses from the parish sought to build on the presentations, to make connections between them and confirmation. They could broadly be summarised along the following lines:

> The values you shared with us are very good values, but you are at a crossroads in life now, moving on from childhood to the teenage years. In those years it will be hard to hold on to your values. Our message for you tonight is that the God that Jesus teaches us about is a God who is on your side as you try to stay true to these values. God made each of you unique, beautiful and gifted, and wants you to be true to your best selves. God is love and made each of you so that you are happiest when you love. In confirmation, God wants to strengthen you

> to be your best selves and to love others. Staying close to God in the coming months and years will help you to do this.

After the response the students were offered quiet, private time to fill in their commitment cards. The commitment cards had questions formulated from the presentations. How will I be true to myself? How will I show love for others? How will I stay close to God? It was clear on each of the nights (seven schools took part) that both students and parents were very engaged by the process. The evaluations subsequently were quite positive. I have no certainty at all about the long-term impact of this approach as opposed to more traditional ways. However, I did find it very uplifting that the challenge of the twelve-year-old boy to move beyond monologue could be met in the context of a parish sacramental programme.

SECTION 2: JUSTICE

CHAPTER

19 Works as well as words

Recently I had a conversation with a young woman working with a Traveller organisation. She was interested in my perspective on church and my reasons for involvement. I spoke happily about the relevance of gospel vision for the culture and the potential of the church as an agent for that vision in modern Ireland. She listened intently and responded without any trace of anger or aggression – yet what she had to say quietened me.

For a number of years she has been a member of organisations combating social discrimination against Travellers. She has a sense of the Traveller organisations as small, having little power, little say in the big issues to do with Traveller health, accommodation, education, employment, discrimination and so on. She has a sense of the church organisations (particularly parishes) being big, carrying weight, but not engaging with these big issues, leaving them instead to the Traveller organisations. She had no sense of the church being with her or being interested in her struggles.

It was clear to me that in her experience my own words on church and gospel values rang hollow. I had to acknowledge to myself the truth of her experience. This is not at all to say that there has been no involvement of church people with social justice issues. We can immediately think of many church people – priests, religious and laity – who have played key roles in various groups struggling for justice. However, their involvement is more the exception than the rule for church. Most of the time most organisations struggling for justice are on the margins of church life, are disconnected from the parishes where they work.

For me this woman's words echo in a powerful and disturbing way the call of John Paul II to show our Christian faith in works as well as in words. He asked us to pay attention to the poor around us, 'groups …threatened by despair at the lack of meaning in their lives, by drug addiction, by fear of abandonment in old age or sickness, by marginalisation or social discrimination'. Without reaching out to these people 'the proclamation of the Gospel, which is itself the prime form of charity, risks being misunderstood or submerged by the ocean of words which daily engulfs us in today's society of mass communications'. He summarises this very aptly: 'The charity of works ensures an unmistakable efficacy to the charity of word…We must therefore ensure that in every Christian community the poor feel at home' *(At the Beginning of the New Millennium,* n. 50).

What does this concretely mean in our parishes? Many priests may feel unable to even touch on this question because they already feel overwhelmed by their present workload. Here one of the huge values of a parish leadership group is that it provides a space within which such questions can be attended to and explored. However, even where such groups exist there may also be a paralysing sense of powerlessness. John Paul offers a key direction out of this inertia. In maintaining the tradition of charity which has been part of the life of the church for two millennia he says that now 'is the time for a new "creativity" in charity, not only by ensuring that help is effective but also by "getting close" to those who suffer, so that the hand that helps is seen not as a humiliating handout but as a sharing between brothers and sisters'.

This says that our first step should be to come close to the marginalised and the organisations that are on their side; to build relationships with them, listen to what they have to say, explore *with them* how the parish might respond. In the coming year much time and energy will rightly be spent in our parishes on our ministries of word – our liturgies, sacraments, homilies and so on. Could we give the same energy to ministries of works? Before another year has passed could we commit ourselves to some initiative that connects us with some marginalised group and with those like the young woman above who work with them? Could she and those like her experience church as being on her side? Could we open ourselves up to whatever possibilities such contact with her may reveal? John Paul doesn't at all equivocate about the necessity of this: '"I was hungry and you gave me food, I was thirsty and you gave me drink, I was a stranger and you welcomed me, I was naked and you clothed me, I was sick and you visited me, I was in prison and you came to me"

(Mt 25:35-37). This Gospel text is not a simple invitation to charity; it is a page of Christology that sheds a ray of light on the mystery of Christ. By these words, no less than by the orthodoxy of her doctrine, the church measures her fidelity as the Bride of Christ.'

CHAPTER
20 Reaching out to the young

I was intrigued by the high level of media coverage given to the world youth gathering in Germany last summer. I was in the United States at the time. The gathering featured daily in the *New York Times*. A friend of mine with a background in youth ministry was contacted by the *Boston Globe* for comment on the significance of the event. In all his years involved with young people this was the first time that the newspaper had sought him out.

Back at home I was asked by a reporter for my views on how the gathering should be followed up: 'What should be put in place for all those young people coming back from Germany?' The question left me a little uneasy. In the reporter's view the German gathering offered a model for youth ministry. It was a spectacular example of the church having the courage to preach the gospel to the young, an example that exposed the lack of such courage generally.

He was certainly right in one respect: there is a fear in parishes regarding youth ministry. While it is a constant feature in discussions at various pastoral gatherings the talk does not often translate into action. Many of the people who have a brief at diocesan level to promote youth ministry activities in parishes are struck by the gap between the high level of 'supply', in terms of the range of youth ministry possibilities available, and the low level of actual demand in the parishes. But I think he was wrong in seeing the gathering as a model for youth ministry, as a kind of 'primary' form that needs a 'secondary' follow-up in the parishes.

The primary form of youth ministry needs to be one that can connect with the masses of the young – not one that will attract and touch only a minority, however large that minority appears on a world stage. I believe that such primary youth ministry is simply the local community witnessing to its faith, offering a lived faith context for the young to grow up in. A youth ministry that can touch young people in the first instance is simply the parish being true to itself. The adult community living quietly and confidently the message 'Love one another as I have loved you'. There is, of course, a dilemma here. In the rapidly changing cultural context it is more difficult for the young to attend to and to read the significance of our Christian living. We are struggling to communicate our religious experience to them. My sense is that the root cause of our difficulty has less to do with the cultural context and more to do with the quality of our own religious experience. I do not mean to be negative or defeatist here. On the contrary: I am saying that youth ministry is within the capacity of every parish community. It is not in the first instance about us trying to change them; it is about us trying to change ourselves.

Beyond that, youth ministry entails us being true to ourselves in a way that is open to and welcoming of the young; a way that is patient with them when they do not appear to be interested in what we offer; a way that stays open to the special moments when the young turn to us, when they have no place else to go. Some time ago I attended a prayer service for a young person seriously injured in an accident. The church was full of people of all ages, including many young who would not normally be there. The rosary was the main prayer used. A young person was invited to lead a decade. Halfway through he stumbled on the words of the Hail Mary and something beautiful happened: the congregation joined in with him, offering him a gentle chorus of support to the end of the decade. I was hugely touched by that moment. For me it was an example of the church and youth ministry at its best.

In making the above point I am not for a moment rejecting the variety of ministry programmes involving groups of young people in discussions, prayer, liturgy, actions, pilgrimage and so on. My point is simply that their contribution is best if it is building on the young people's experience of parish, if they are following up on what is happening in the parish. What happens in the parishes is the priority that these gatherings can be in reference to. High profile youth gatherings such as that in Germany should not make us lose sight of this priority. Youth ministry starts at home, with the adults.

CHAPTER

21 Listening at the margins

It is a very arresting sign of the times that those on the margins of Irish society are also on the margins of the church. The majority of contemporary poor people in Ireland belong to the 'A' group. I also find it very interesting that a great many people involved in various kinds of development work among marginalised groups are also in the 'A' group. There are, of course, many church people who have committed their whole lives to working in and with marginalised communities. However, it is clear that our church system on the whole is marginal in such communities. Most of our pastoral approaches simply do not work. These approaches are based on a standardised delivery of a range of pastoral services, irrespective of the life circumstances of the people. For decades we have gone on delivering those services without any fundamental evaluation, even though patently there is something not connecting.

I believe this situation requires a fundamental shift in practice. I would like to explore what that shift might look like in relation to our rituals among communities on the margins. These rituals represent a notable tension point in the church at present. Most of the time, the majority of the people in such communities ignore our rituals, except on special occasions. These occasions, of course, are very familiar – birth, marriage, death, first communion, confirmation. We are very concerned as to how we deal with this situation. Is it possible to honour both the rituals and the people? I think it is. I believe the key fundamental shift we need to make is very simple: *listen to the experience of the people and reshape the language and symbols of our rituals so that they more effectively communicate the presence of God to that experience.*

While this is simple to express, it is less easy to do. It requires in the first instance a mind shift, but also a shift in practice. Here I think the theory and practice of Paulo Freire is very evocative. An adult educator among marginalised people in Brazil, Freire struggled to break through the apathy that arose from their experience. He believed that the struggle to attain a fully human life is part of the human vocation, and is part of what makes us human. He never lost sight of the dignity of the people. He remained convinced that people can challenge the circumstances that marginalise them; they can work to change their lives. For him agency was a key implication of dignity. For this reason his key question was never, 'How do we help people?' but, 'How do we help people to help themselves?'.

He developed a set of key principles and practices that shaped his education work:
1 The way we work with people is never neutral; it is either helping them to challenge the status quo or it is maintaining the status quo

2 People will act on issues around which they have strong feelings now – emotion is closely connected to motivation
3 Because people are thinking, creative beings with the capacity for action the most appropriate way of education and development is problem-posing – giving people the opportunity to explore the issues they have strong feelings on, drawing out their insights and feelings
4 None of us is as smart as all of us – dialogue is the most effective way of building up insight, not monologue
5 Reflection on issues of concern followed by action, followed by reflection on the action and so on is the most effective way of enabling people to address their own situation.

Freire's theory shaped in turn his practice. The foundation stone of all his work was listening to the people whom he hoped to touch. Freire suggests a very concrete approach. I have touched on his 'listening survey' earlier (see Chapter 14). Because people will only act on issues around which they have strong feelings, it is vital for education work to start by listening to these. What are people angry, sad, hurt, worried, delighted about?

I believe that the same approach could inform our work of evangelisation. I believe there is enormous scope for the building up of a church of the people in marginalised communities *if* the principles and method above are respected; *if* the core task is seen in terms of developing a conversation between the life concerns of the people and the good news of the gospel; *if* we church people recognise that we lack the tools to communicate effectively that good news; *if* we recognise that we will only find those tools in a genuine partnership with the marginalised people themselves. I do not underestimate the depth of conversion that such would require of us.

I will flesh out an example of what I have in mind. Some time ago I was involved in a listening survey among a group of young parents living in a marginalised community with major drug problems. The parents simply talked to each other about their lives and the fundamental issues that were concerning them in the rearing of their children. For me it was an awe-full experience in both senses of the word. It was an encounter with extraordinary depth; a depth of vision about the uniqueness and sacredness of their children, about their children's right to lives that are whole, happy and healthy; a depth of love that drives them to struggle against huge odds to protect their children; a depth of pain in the face of the constant difficulties and failures in this struggle.

A number of burning questions surfaced for the parents out of this depth. How do we maintain our own health in body and spirit in the face of this struggle? How can we maintain communications and good relationships with our children as they grow towards their teens so that we can know what is going on in their lives and be a support to them? How do we relate to those in our community who seek to hurt our children and would hurt us if we publicly challenged them? How do we deal with the broader society and its agencies that look down on us and our children?

Earlier I was suggesting a broad orientation for us as church in twenty-first century culture – find the traces of the Spirit and follow them. Is there not a trace of the Spirit in the depth of these parents? And what does evangelisation mean in this context if not an encounter between this depth and the depth of the gospel? The good news that their vision for their children is the truth; that God is with them in their struggle; that the church is a body of people to whom they and their children can belong – a body that understands and is willing to engage with their burning questions.

What are the opportunities for such evangelisation? What are the entry points for church into the lives of these people? For most, church exists on the edge of their lives and consciousness, except on special occasions including the birth of a child – a moment of extraordinary poignancy that marks the beginning of many years of hope and struggle. If the gospel has enough breadth and depth to embrace the lives and struggles of such as these people, could not our sacrament of Baptism do the same? Is it beyond our imagination to root that sacrament in the context of their lives and struggles? To adapt the language and symbols of the ritual so that it effectively expresses their reality and the good news of the gospel for that reality?

It seems to me that there is huge scope here for pastoral explorations around such key moments where the lives of people at the margins of church and society intersect with church. There are of course many other questions about how the church can be with them in their struggle. Freire's basic approach is that we explore these questions with the people, not for them. Only in the context of real partnership will the answers emerge.

Baptism could be a start. A powerful, symbolic moment where the good news of the gospel is heard in language and symbols that speak to the deepest, most sacred spaces in the hearts of the most marginal in our culture.

SECTION 3: COMMUNION

CHAPTER

22 The priest and managing ministry

One of the very positive signs of the times in the Irish church is the increased awareness among clergy of the need for new pastoral practices to complement the old. I believe this represents a genuine aspiration among a great many clergy, but an aspiration that does not inevitably, or perhaps even often, lead to action. Why the gap between aspiration and action when it comes to developing new ministries? It seems to me that what is very often absent among priests is a sense of the need for a practical strategy for the management of new ministries.

There is something deeply ingrained in clerical culture that resists the concept of managing ministry. A priest friend of mine articulated this resistance very well when he told me that he did not have time to be going to all the meetings that would be entailed in establishing a proposed youth ministry program for the parish. He said he wanted to be out visiting the people. It seemed to me that he was operating out of a deeply committed but almost exclusively personalised understanding of ministry. By this I mean that he had reduced his concept of ministry in the parish to what he himself could do with the time and the gifts that were available to him. He had little space in his imagination for the possibility that there were others in the parish with vocations as well, different to but complementary to his. He had little energy for the messy work of calling, forming and sustaining these other vocations in the parish for ministry.

Essentially, this is what I understand managing ministry to be about – seeking to create conditions that allow for multiple ministries to be carried out simultaneously by as many people as have the necessary gifts and commitment. Because the priest is the full-time church official in the parish, whether he likes it or not, he has an inevitable role in either facilitating or blocking the emergence of such ministries.

Basically, managing ministry is about addressing deeply and in a sustained manner four key questions:

1 *What* are the key ministry needs in the parish?
2 *Who* are the people with potential for these ministries in this parish?
3 *Where* are the resources available to equip them for their ministries?
4 *How* do we connect the people to the resources in order to release their potential?

It seems to me that these are questions that the priest needs to hold close to his heart during the bits and pieces of his day-to-day work; always seeking to discern needs and gifts in the parish, always paying attention to supports and resources coming on stream within or beyond the parish that may be relevant to these. Managing ministry is about staying alive to these questions in the midst of the multiple demands on the priest's time. It is not about becoming swamped by them but slowly, gradually, one at a time, proactively responding to the opportunities as they are revealed. I believe there are more people available to minister to real felt needs than we give credit for and there are far more resources available (often not very expensively) to equip these people than we are aware of. What is often lacking are people who will discern the potential ministers, spot the opportunities for formation and put energy into connecting the two.

My conviction is that a crucial enabling step in all this is the formation of a parish leadership group (generally called parish pastoral councils) that can carry with the priest this management role. Here the leadership group functions like a gardener – it identifies the suitable soil, plants the seeds, provides some support for the growing plants. However, it is the seeds themselves that have to grow and produce fruit!

If such a group is in place and functioning I believe this can have a hugely liberating effect on the work of the priest. If there is a collective management of ministry development it creates space for the priest to look at his own role. Some time ago I met with a group of priests who were exploring the possibility of employing a pastoral coordinator. They asked me about my own experience in the work. I showed them my work contract, which included a description of my areas of responsibility and system of accountability. One priest responded wistfully, saying, 'I wish I had a contract like that, with a clear sense of where my responsibility begins and ends and someone to be accountable to'. I could certainly relate to how he was feeling. I remembered being in the role of a pastoral coordinator some years earlier without the job description (or even a job title!). I found it very stressful and exhausting – I did not know whether I was doing a good job or even what a good job would look like. But then I had my list of priorities – I could tick off what was done and what was not done. I knew whether I was doing more or less than I was supposed to and I had somebody to review this with on a regular basis. I found great freedom in this and great security.

Is it possible and appropriate for a priest to work to a 'neat' job description? I would say 'yes' on both counts. I would also say that as priests become older and fewer, and the pastoral situation more complex, it will be all the more necessary to have a concrete and manageable set of priorities. However, developing such requires a bit of time and space for work planning. Many priests that I know give little time for that. They work hard but mostly in a reactive, overwhelmed sort of way – nearly always with more on their plate than they can reasonably handle. And when they take a break from work the last thing they want to do is talk about work!

I am going to suggest a simple exercise that a priest could do, ideally with the help of a couple of people well clued into his work situation. Draw up a list of all the ministries operating or needed in the parish. Divide the list into two columns headed respectively 'My work' and 'Other people's work'. In the first column, put down the core things you feel that you must do as a priest and add to that anything you really enjoy doing. Put all the rest into the other column. The first column will need to be small enough to allow you time and energy to address the question (with the council), 'How will we empower others to do their work?' How small could or should the 'My work' column be? I will respond to this question with a story.

***

Some time ago Kilkerrin Parish pastoral council were given responsibility for the running of the parish while its priest, the late Fr Sean Higgins, went on a short sabbatical. They had drawn up a list of all the jobs that were to be done in the parish and who was to do them. They liaised with neighbouring priests for masses on some weekdays, for weekend liturgies, funerals, baptisms, weddings and Easter ceremonies. After Sean returned I met with the group again to review their experience. They were delighted with how things had worked out and how well they functioned in the absence of the priest. The various parish ministry groups had continued to function, communion services were organised during the weeks, liturgies still happened at the weekends and the Easter ceremonies went off fine. Parish buildings were opened and closed and repaired as needed. So I asked the question, 'Was the priest missed?' 'Yes,' they said. 'The empty priest's house was a sad sight.' I asked, 'And what was he missed for?' The replied, 'He was missed when there were people in the parish sick. He was missed when people in the parish died.'

Ministry to the sick and the bereaved were identified by this group as core to the priest's work – everything else they could manage themselves with some support from neighbouring parishes. I find this story deeply suggestive in regard to the core function of priests. I am not trying to say what priests should or should not have under their column headed 'My work'. What I am saying is that this column could be smaller, more focused and more manageable for many priests than is currently the case. I am also saying that a reduced workload under the first column would allow more time and energy for making the second column happen.

CHAPTER

23 Parish leadership groups

I take Donal Harrington's article on pastoral councils in *The Furrow* (1999) as my starting point. He identifies the key role of the council as the parish leadership group. It is the group that holds the whole parish in its view, assessing the strengths and weaknesses of the parish as it carries out its mission, and planning for the future in the light of this. Essentially, the council is the place where the key questions facing the parish can be thought about, prayed with, discussed and decided on. It is the place for gathering and expressing the *sensus fidelium* as represented by the members in regard to these questions.

Most groups find such a broad role difficult to manage and tend to move towards specific, contained projects that they can get their teeth into. There is a wisdom in this, in that it meets two survival needs of groups: to have a definite task and to make progress. However, for the pastoral council a real problem arises if the group becomes totally identified with and absorbed by a particular project. It is then no longer the leadership group with an overview

PARISH LEADERSHIP GROUPS

of the whole; it is a parish ministry group with an undoubtedly valuable but still partial focus.

The SEE–JUDGE–ACT method

I would like to suggest here a process by which a pastoral council can hold onto its overview role while at the same time identifying some specific, manageable projects. Here I am drawing on the basic SEE–JUDGE–ACT approach.

SEE

Take a simple framework for looking at the overall parish situation:
- What are the things happening in this parish to proclaim and celebrate our faith (liturgy, sacraments, youth ministry, adult religious education etc.)?
- What are the things happening in this parish to live out our faith (building community, taking care of those who are hurting etc.)?

JUDGE

This means to come to a shared sense of the pastoral priorities to be addressed:
- What are the strengths and weaknesses of each of these as they are done in the parish right now? What are we doing really well? What are the biggest gaps / unmet needs?
- In the light of our analysis, are there a limited number of priorities that we want to and are able to address in this coming year?

ACT
This is more about arranging and making sure that action happens rather than the council taking on operational responsibility directly:
- Can we organise action on these in such a way as to include others not in this group?
- What will we have done by when?

The above set of questions could provide the agenda for an initial series of meetings at the beginning of a year or of a three-year term. The value of the above approach is that it provides a very definite framework for a pastoral council to carry out its overview and planning function, while at the same time allowing it to move towards specific projects. Because the projects are identified within a definite and recurring framework of planning and evaluation, the group (hopefully!) does not lose sight of its overall leadership role.

Who are the best people to be on the council and how are they to be recruited? My conviction is that the best people are 'ordinary' parishioners; people who have a feel for their faith and a feel for the community that constitutes the parish. Not people with any special expertise or even special involvements, but people who want to see church and faith as part of the future of their parish and are willing to put some time and energy into planning with others for that future. I believe that the best way of finding such people is simply to call them to come forward of their own accord. A homily at the weekend masses and an explanatory leaflet delivered to all homes can outline the purpose of the council, the commitment entailed and the qualities needed. People can be asked to offer themselves for the role. A short orientation programme for those that come forward can then allow the organising committee and the volunteers to discern whether or not the role of the council is suitable for them. This is an important practical question, as the process outlined above is vulnerable to abuse by a person who has a particular agenda and who might see the council as a vehicle for carrying through what the individual has already decided the parish needs.

Most councils meet at most once or twice a month for two hours at a time amounting to between twenty and forty hours of meeting time per year. If the role for the council is to provide the overall leadership and direction for the parish, it is clear that the time available for this role is a very valuable and scarce resource. That time needs to be managed carefully to optimise the effectiveness of the council (getting the job done) and its efficiency (not wasting people's time and energy).

It is a huge advantage to have a small steering group to manage the general agenda of the parish pastoral council. So, for example, if one of the priorities of the council is to assess how liturgy is conducted in the parish, a discussion on the Easter ceremonies could be pencilled in for the January meeting. This approach has a double advantage: it allows plenty of time to identify and gather in whatever information is needed for a fruitful discussion and it allows time for follow-up action in advance of Easter. In this same way a range of key issues could be distributed in advance over a number of council meetings.

The steering committee can also plan the specific agenda for the coming meeting. Planning the agenda means more than identifying a list of items for discussion. It also means clarifying the purpose of having the particular items on the agenda and how best to structure the time and the discussion in order to achieve that purpose.

I was a member of a pastoral council for a number of years and we found the following structure very helpful:

1 Start directly with the main item in order to ensure that it gets the time it needs. We used to find that the discussion on minutes, matters arising and correspondence could eat into huge chunks of the meeting, leaving too little time for the planned item.
2 Build the prayer into the discussion of the main item. We used to start our meetings with the prayer – with reflective music, candles and silence. Invariably some people would arrive late and disturb the quiet atmosphere. So we put it back to the middle of the discussion and found (by accident) that its impact was much more powerful. We found it much easier for the group to be present to the prayer. Having it in the middle of our work was a vivid reminder of whose work it was we were doing.
3 Have minutes, matters arising, correspondence etc. at the end of the meeting. We found that we could still get through these, even when there was limited time left. And we always stopped at closing time for a cup of tea!

To ensure a follow-through on decisions it is important that some simple, procedural structures are in place.

1 Decisions need to be recorded in a format that specifies
   - what was decided
   - who is responsible for what resultant action by when
2 The steering group of the council needs to meet between meetings to plan for the coming meeting and to monitor the follow-through from the previous meeting.

The preparation for the council meetings takes time but I believe that the time taken is more than compensated for by the time saved at the meetings. In a culture where the time of volunteers is becoming a scarcer resource, it is imperative that we do not waste that time, particularly when it comes to such a key resource as the members of the parish pastoral council.

CHAPTER 24

Structure and spirituality for communion

The council needs a discipline in regard to how the meetings are prepared and run. This discipline needs to be facilitated, not by an outside 'expert', but by one or more of the council members who have some capacity for facilitation. I have mentioned the value of identifying a limited number of priority issues for the council to address and distributing those issues over a number of meetings. This gives time for some necessary preparations to allow the council to have a fruitful discussion on the issues.

Crucial here is information. I have also suggested that the ideal membership for a council are people who are not 'experts' in any particular pastoral area. It follows that they will need relevant information if they are to be able to offer their sense of what needs to be done. So, for example, if the council prioritised outreach to young parents, it would be very helpful for the members to know what kind of outreaches are being tried and tested elsewhere before having to make a decision on what will be done in their own parish.

STRUCTURE AND SPIRITUALITY FOR COMMUNION

I have found that the following format for a discussion on the priority issue has been very fruitful:

1 *Sharing of relevant information.* One or more people are asked to have gathered for the meeting the information necessary for the council to have an informed discussion.
2 *Allowing opportunity for clarification.* If the purpose of the meeting is to gather the *sensus fidelium* it is vital that each member feels able to contribute and is given the space to ask whatever questions they feel will be helpful for this contribution.
3 *Bringing the core question to prayer.* I have found over and over again that well-prepared prayer, lasting ten to fifteen minutes in the middle of the meeting, brings an extra depth and quality to the discussion and creates a much better environment for listening and sharing.
4 *Hearing the views of each member.* It is central to the function of the council that each member is listened to, and the facilitation has to attend carefully to this. Practically speaking, this means asking, 'Can we hear now from those who have not had the chance to speak yet?'
5 *Identifying the pattern in the sharing.* This is about noticing the consensus coming through and trusting that where ordinary people of faith come together to listen, to pray and to share about a significant pastoral question, and where there is substantial agreement coming through in regard to what to do, such agreement does express the *sensus fidelium*.
6 *Taking a decision.* The council needs to have the courage to act decisively on its sense – to identify what needs to be done now, by whom and by when.

The pastoral council is the place where the key pastoral questions facing the parish are explored in a prayerful and decisive manner. Two key elements of the functioning of the council are held together in this understanding. On the one hand, the council is a reflective body that is prepared to gather around questions for which there are no immediately obvious answers. On the other hand, the council is an action body that takes and follows through on decisions, seeing the resultant actions as essential raw materials for its ongoing reflective role.

This action–reflection dynamic requires a level of self-confidence in the council body, which is often lacking among the parishioner-members who are fearful of how the people will react to a council initiative. This fear can lead to an endless, energy-sapping round of consultations, surveys, public meetings and so on. I am not at all suggesting that the council should never consult, but I do think a sensible balance needs to be held here. If the council members are of the people, if they have a genuine feel for their community and their faith, if they follow together a prayerful, structured approach to their reflection then on most issues they should trust in their own common sense and act on it. Here the parish priest can play a very important role in affirming and encouraging the council members towards such self-confidence.

Of course, this very confidence can be missing in the parish priest, who may be fearful of what decisions the council might seek to make and may not trust either the members or the process sufficiently to embark on a prayerful and decisive exploration of key pastoral questions. Given his canonical responsibilities he may feel precluded from putting himself into a position where he has to account for actions with which he does not agree.

Some time ago I found this question being highlighted in a very interesting way at a conference on pastoral renewal in the United States. The participants were predominantly Protestant pastoral theologians, lay and clerical. I was happily telling them about the increased lay involvement in the Irish church and the emergence of various structures for lay participation in decision making.

While being generally positive about this, they also sounded a note of warning about the danger of a lay authoritarian model of parish. They had experience in their churches of situations where authority rested with lay councils and where the councils used that authority to effectively block parish clergy from taking initiatives the councils did not approve of. The picture they painted was familiar: a conservative, authoritarian parish leadership opposed to and preventing any unfamiliar approaches to parish renewal. The only difference was that the leadership in their case was lay rather than clerical.

While the possibility of this scenario developing here seems remote, I find the comments of the conference stimulating. The exciting possibility for parish pastoral councils is that they will find a way of working that respects the charism, experience and insights of both priests and people; a way of working that does not seek to make one subservient to the other; a way that looks to create a genuine partnership of charisms, working together in mutual respect.

While this might sound very idealistic, it offers a positive way of dealing with the question of authority and decision making. Authority in the pastoral council does not lie either with the priests or with the people, but in the spirit of their relationship. Where the relationship is not one of a deep, mutual respect, the council will be crippled anyway. No amount of work on a legal constitution will make up for it. The focus needs to be first on the spirit rather than the law.

My understanding of the structured process outlined above is that it offers a very practical framework for a genuine partnership of people and priests. It avoids the extremes of either the priest taking decisions against the wishes of the people or the people doing likewise with the priest. Where there is a genuine atmosphere of trust and listening between both parties, where there is a common search for the *sensus fidelium* as expressed by the whole group, then if either party has strong, conscientious difficulties with a proposed decision, that is sufficient reason for the council not to take that decision. This means going back to the question again until there is a decision coming forward that priest and people together can support. My experience of being on a council over the years is that this approach works very well once there is a prayerful and open spirit among the members.

I will summarise here what are for me the crucial challenges of a council in terms of its spirituality:
1. *Nurturing faith.* The core sense of unity and energy of the pastoral council is that we are here together doing God's work. Bringing reflective, participative prayer

into the heart of each meeting keeps us in touch with that sense.

2 *Nurturing trust and respect.* This means putting into practice the faith that the God whom we serve is among us, speaking and acting through each and all. Practically, this means the meetings being facilitated in such a way as to optimise the opportunities for everyone to contribute and be listened to.

3 *Nurturing patience.* This involves realising that as we are developing a new way of being a church, it will take time to learn how to do it well. We will need to be gentle with ourselves and one another as we try to move forward. This means planning a workload that is reasonable and realistic for the present capacity of the group, and also regular evaluations that put as much emphasis on encouragement as criticism.

4 *Nurturing a sense of humour.* Taking God's work seriously does not mean that we have to take ourselves too seriously. Creating an atmosphere where laughter and fun fit easily makes a huge contribution to the group sustaining its focus and energy, and surviving its difficulties.

It takes generosity and courage for priests and people to embark on the journey towards partnership in parish. There is no good reason why that journey in all its up and downs shouldn't be life giving for all involved.

CHAPTER

25 Organising for action

In looking at the action follow-through to council decisions, strong consideration needs to be given to the question of who, outside of the council membership, has the potential to be involved in the action. My experience is that there is on the ground in parishes a significant resource of people who have a passion for particular pastoral issues. Part of the action planning is to find ways of identifying and calling forward such people.

I believe this is a crucial issue that any council will need to address – finding a way of addressing pastoral priorities on an ongoing basis that enables effective delegation of tasks. For each pastoral priority identified a group of parishioners who have energy for that issue need to be identified and equipped to take responsibility for it. This way the council does not become cluttered with or weighed down by an increasing operational workload. It keeps 'clearing the decks' so that it can continue with its fundamental leadership role in the parish – to be the place where the key questions facing the parish are identified, explored and addressed.

ORGANISING FOR ACTION

I will suggest here a framework for delegation of tasks that I have found very effective in the past:

- *Step 1* – identify a concrete way of addressing the particular pastoral need. Most potential volunteers are nervous about being asked to tackle a question if there is no clear answer to begin with. I remember being involved some years ago in recruiting adult volunteers for retreat work with teenagers. Our first step was to design a very specific half-day programme as a clear example of what we wanted the adults to do, and how they could do it.
- *Step 2* – invite the potential volunteers to an information event where they have the opportunity (no strings attached) to see exactly what it is they are being asked to do. It is vital that they know in advance that this is a 'come and see' gathering – they are free to look at the task and say 'no'. Our potential volunteers would have been too nervous to come to the information night if they thought that they were going to be pressurised to get involved in the retreat work.
- *Step 3* – invite those interested to take part in a training programme that will equip them to take on the task. What I have found helpful here was to be able to say to the potential volunteers, 'Do the training. You'll enjoy it. When the training is completed you can then decide whether or not you want to take on the task.' So for each step there is an 'out'. Our potential volunteers all thought that the retreat proposal was a great idea, but not for them! They only went ahead with the training on the clear understanding that they would not be obliged to do the retreat work.

- *Step 4* – invite those who have completed the training to take on the task for a specified period, normally a year. In the case above the adults developed a new confidence in the training that they could take on the task. They were willing to commit for a definite period.
- *Step 5* – at the end of the agreed period invite the volunteers who have engaged with the task to an evaluation. Here they look back on their experience and their learnings. They are invited to redesign the way of working that was given to them. At this point they are invited to consider a further period of commitment to the task. So what was originally handed to them as a 'package' they are now redesigning themselves; they are taking ownership of it. In the example above the adults returned with a great sense of achievement: they had completed the retreat task; they had insights into how the task could be done better; and they had the energy to keep going.

The above can be summarised in the diagram overleaf. From the point of view of the potential volunteer the starting point is an information night, which leads on to a training event, which in turn leads to the action, all of which concludes with the evaluation. The commitment is now completed and the volunteer is free to move away or to return for another cycle. From the point of view of the group coordinating this process the starting point is in identifying a feasible, concrete action to meet some prioritised need. The second step is to identify a training programme that can equip potential volunteers to undertake the action. The third step is to organise an information event that promotes both the action and the training.

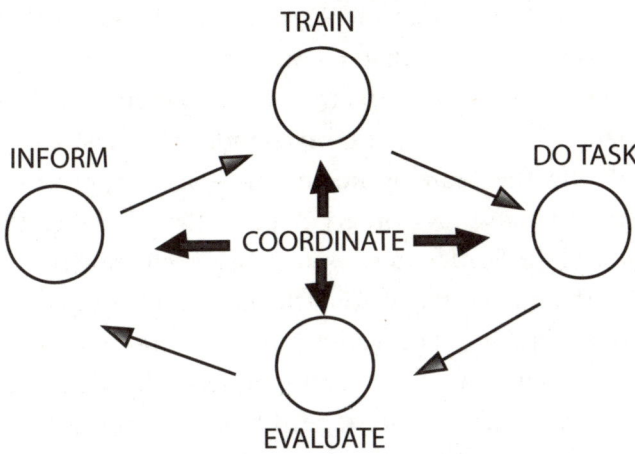

Learning how to offer the gift of the gospel in our new culture is a challenge that requires the energy and gifts of all who are willing to minister in the church. In our parishes and dioceses we need to create confident, competent teams of people who can engage in ministry, draw wisdom from the engagement, communicate that wisdom – and in all this enjoy what they are doing. Such groups correspond in business jargon to high-performance teams – highly motivated, self-directed groups that can function within the broader goals of the organisation.

It may seem odd in that context that the above model starts with an answer. It seems to be spoon feeding the volunteers. It seems authoritarian in its approach of telling the volunteers what to do. What is important to recognise here is that this approach seeks to end up with confident, competent teams of volunteers for parish ministries; it does not presume that we start with these.

Kenneth Blancard's *The One Minute Manager Builds High Performance Teams* (1992) explores the rationale for this approach in a way that I find very helpful. Blanchard recognises four stages in the development of high-performance teams and four corresponding leadership roles. At stage one the team is beginning – its competence is necessarily low and its primary need is for clear direction. The role of the leader here is to offer such direction. At stage two the team is engaged in the task and has discovered its lack of experience. The leadership task at this point is very intensive – being with the team in its task, supporting, encouraging, coaching. At stage three, once the team has survived its initial difficulties, its experience and ability will have grown, with a corresponding increase in its confidence. It still needs the support of the leader, but to a significantly lesser extent. At stage four the team is competent and confident. The appropriate leadership style is now delegation. Let them get on with the task themselves.

My own experience in seeking to develop church ministries is that we frequently make one of two opposite mistakes. The first is that we never truly delegate. Whether the leadership is the priest or the council, we seek to hold on to the reins of control of a particular ministry or ministry group when that group is more than competent of doing the business itself. The second is that we seek to delegate too soon. Presenting a group of volunteers with a particular issue and expecting them to discover and implement a solution by themselves. We leave them to sink or swim and, generally, they sink.

ORGANISING FOR ACTION

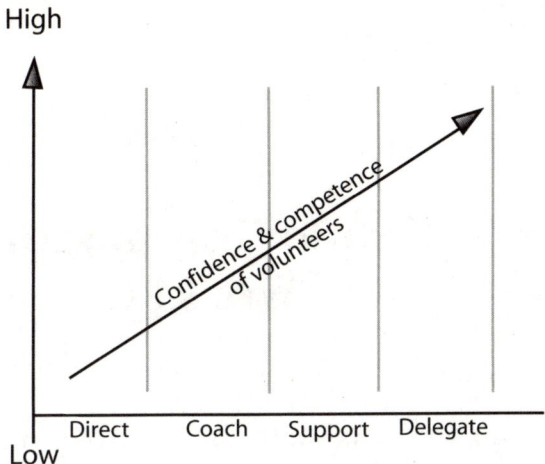

Leadership style needed by volunteers

I think the above model is very realistic and respectful in regard to volunteers. It recognises their potential for confident, competent leadership, but it also recognises the support they need to achieve that potential. Delegation is eventually arrived at, but through stages of direction, coaching and support.

I appreciate that the above framework is somewhat elaborate. It can, of course, be adapted to local circumstances, but I believe it provides a helpful way for councils to think about how they might go about setting up self-sufficient working groups.

CHAPTER

26 Employing pastoral workers

Over the years I have met with a number of parishes that are actively considering the employment of a parish pastoral coordinator. They see this as a necessary move because of two pastoral realities. On the one hand, the need to put more time and energy into the calling, forming and sustaining of lay people for ministry in the parish; on the other hand, the reduction in the number of priests available to do this work. However, it seems likely that, at least for the present, only a minority of parishes will seriously consider this move. While most accept the need for greater lay involvement in the delivery of a wider range of parish ministries, few see the employment of a pastoral coordinator as a realistic option – because of the question of money. Most parishes feel they cannot afford it.

I accept that generally parishes could not afford to employ a pastoral coordinator if they are thinking in terms of a full-time, permanent, pensionable position. Even if they could afford it many would still be reluctant to go that way because of fears of what might happen down the road. However, there are other, more flexible and less expensive ways of buying in pastoral workers. Charles Handy is a well-known and very astute commentator on global work patterns. He sees the future of work as more and more the worker finding customers rather than employers. By this he means that from now on more people will need to identify and develop skills they can offer, services they can supply to organisations. Instead of asking the organisations to employ them they will be asking the organisations to buy their skills and services as needed. Hence the customer rather than the employer relationship.

I think there is something here for parishes to pay attention to. Within this model of work the question is not, 'Can we afford to employ a worker?' but, 'How many hours can we afford to contract in somebody with what skills to do what pastoral work?' My own work as a pastoral coordinator was exactly on that basis. The parish judged it could afford to contract me in for a thousand hours in the year to cover a specified area of work. It could equally have decided to contract me in for one hundred hours. The parish solicitor drew up the contract. In it I was held to be self-employed. I was responsible for my own tax, PRSI and travel costs. The parish could terminate my contract at a month's notice and had no further obligations to me. For my part I was a free agent outside the thousand hours and could sell my time and skills to whoever else wanted to buy them.

While there is nothing new in this model for church work (people involved in giving retreats, missions and novenas have been at it for years), it seems to me that there is great potential in its further development so that there could be available to parishes a range of pastoral resource people whom the parishes could avail of as they needed and could afford. This would keep the onus on the resource people to keep developing their skills and services in the light of the changing needs of parishes.

This, of course, raises the question, 'Where are these resource people to come from?' There are, I believe, quite a number already available and perhaps a register of who they are and what they have to offer might be useful now. There are a number of colleges with pastoral ministry programmes of one kind or another. A parish, a number of parishes or a diocese could sponsor one or more individuals to do one of these programmes, not on the basis that they would subsequently be employed, but on the basis that there will be some contract work available for them.

Some people have raised the question of the justice of this approach to work. I do not think that there is any injustice in the concept of parishes providing opportunities for self-employed pastoral people to provide pastoral services. We do this all the time with other service providers such as builders, accountants and so on. There is a certain risk taking involved for the pastoral worker, but it seems to me inevitable, given the emerging situation of the church here, that there will be loads of work available for those who can provide practical pastoral services that respond effectively to some of the many needs of today's parishes.

CHAPTER

27 'Expectant' leadership

There are moments in the midst of change and decay when we tap into a deeper sense in ourselves, not just of hope, but of expectation; expectation that sooner or later things must turn for the church. Not back to where we were, but forward to a time when the Christian vision is a fresh, creative, wave-making presence in the culture; when it has again the capacity to turn the heads and spark the imagination of ordinary people; when they welcome church as a bearer of gifts for their flourishing.

We already know, perhaps if only from echoes deep in our souls, that the gospel message is too beautiful for this never to happen. We know that whatever about the frantic pace of popular culture there remains a quieter space in people's hearts where the gospel can take root. We know too that despite our brokenness as church there are still great numbers among us – priests, religious and laity – who would with a heart and a half be willing bearers of the gospel in today's culture if we could. And we know, if nothing else, that the Spirit is already at work in all this, preparing for the new even as the old collapses. This is a combustible mix, for sure. We would love to know from where might come the spark to set it ablaze. And, of course, we do not know, except for this: it will not come from somewhere else; it will come from among us, from our Spirit-prompted efforts. We will not hear those prompts if we are in panic or despair; we will hear them, no matter what noise is around us, if we can hold this calm, expectant space; a space alert for possibilities and opportunities; a space confident, that sooner or later, we will find effective ways of carrying out our mission; a space which frees us to move in measured, exploratory steps into the deep.

That space is especially important for leadership in our parishes. Not just personal, individual space, though it includes that, but group space. At its heart that is what a pastoral council is: a group seeking to be in touch with its own Spirit expectation; a group that draws from this the courage to be calm. It is out of such a space that the council can fulfil its mission. That mission is simple if enormous: through a process of trial and error to spark parish initiatives that enable people experience the warmth of the good news of the gospel; initiatives old and new, in works as well as in words, and carried out in a spirit of communion; initiatives that of themselves may be intensive and hectic, but arise out of the calm, prayerful rhythm of SEE–JUDGE-ACT. To 'see' means to look carefully at the reality of parish life from the viewpoint of both faith and justice (words and works). What are the needs and possibilities in terms of faith development? What are the needs and possibilities in terms of reaching out to people who are hurting? To 'judge' means to 'land' on a limited number of priorities for the coming period through a prayerful process of listening and sharing. To 'act' means to see that initiatives are attempted in the parish, drawing on the energies and gifts of the wider parish in the same spirit of communion as shapes the working of the council. That action, no matter how it turns out, becomes itself a rich source for further fruitful reflection.

Movement and action is essential in our mission. We engage with the choppy pastoral waters of our time and place but with a calm, expectant spirit.

References

Blanchard, Kenneth, *The One Minute Manager Builds High Performance Teams* (Harper Collins: 1992).

Donovan, Vincent, *Christianity Rediscovered* (Orbis: 2005).

Handy, Charles, *The Empty Raincoat* (London, Hutchinson: 1990).

Harrington, Donal, 'Parish Pastoral Councils', *The Furrow*, May 1999.

McNamara, Vincent, *New Life for Old: On Desire and Becoming Human* (Columba Press: 2004).